OSHKOSH MEMORIES

OSHKOSH MEMORIES

Reflections on the World's Greatest Fly-In

Stories Collected by
Jill Rutan Hoffman

Writers Club Press
San Jose · New York · Lincoln · Shanghai

Oshkosh Memories

Reflections on the World's Greatest Fly-In

Published by Writers Club Press
an imprint of iUniverse.com, Inc.

For information address:
iUniverse.com, Inc.
620 North 48th Street
Suite 201
Lincoln, NE 68504-3467
www.iuniverse.com

ISBN: 0-595-00602-7

Printed in the United States of America

To the Young Eagles, especially Noelle and Haley.

May your lives be flights of fancy that fulfill your wildest dreams

EPIGRAPH

◆

Young Eagles

Let us not wring our hands in despair.

Let us use our hands to repair a sagging

spirit—a fading work ethic.

Let us build a foundation, a firm ground

of belief in our youth.

Let us give them the tools to create their

own future, and in so doing—enhance

the future of aviation in America.

Let us support their efforts—that they

may support themselves.

Let us not decry what "Might have been",

but rejoice in what is—what can be—

if we so will it to be.

◆

◆

Let us ignore the nay sayers.

Let us be the yea-sayers.

Let us raise our heads—our eyes and

our hearts—to the skies above—that we

may soar like eagles.

◆

Eagles—vigilant.

Eagles—determined.

Eagles—young.

Written and Donated by Cliff Robertson

◆

Contents

FOREWORD

So often, when I hear someone talking about AirVenture Oshkosh, their words are all about objects: 12,000 planes, 750 exhibitors, 500 forums, Pioneer Airport, AirVenture Museum, and so on. Which is fine. All are important and integral parts of our annual weeklong celebration of aviation, all reasons for its ongoing popularity and continued success.

My point, however, is that we should never forget that the real key to the success of not only AirVenture Oshkosh the event, but EAA the organization, is its people. EAA is made up of thousands upon thousands of loyal and hardworking members who, because of their collective love of flying, return to Oshkosh to attend and/or participate each year. EAA is more than just an organization. It is also a community of people, who have not only shared a common experience over the years, but become close friends as well.

That's why I'm so enthused about Jill Rutan Hoffman's remarkable new book, "Oshkosh Memories". Because in it, she relates, through the stories of others, that special and genuine enthusiasm EAA members have not just for airplanes—but also for each other. Of all the benefits of EAA membership, it is perhaps the most intangible, and yet certainly one of the most valuable and long lasting. Jill's book reflects the desires and hopes that unite EAA members—famous and commonplace—and the passion they have for their sport.

A songwriter once wrote, "Every picture tells a story.". In Jill's book, every story paints a small picture, one of thousands that make up the broad spectrum of human experience that is AirVenture. The recollections are alternately humorous, intriguing, touching, and exciting—but ultimately very rewarding. Because they give us all a chance to do what we do when we return to AirVenture each summer—to share experiences of other EAA members, experiences that bind us closer together over the years.

One of the most important things we have is our memories. They are not always the most significant things we do, but the little things we do that later become significant in our mind for whatever reasons. As time passes, the value of those memories increases along with the people we meet. For myself, I can only say that EAA has allowed me to meet many wonderful people, and share in their experiences our common love of flying. In "Oshkosh Memories" Jill allows me to renew old acquaintances, and make some new friends as well.

Sincerely,
Tom Poberezny
President, EAA

ACKNOWLEDGEMENTS

This book took almost two years from the time my husband and I came up with the idea to the book's completion. Some would commend me for taking on such a large task but in reality it was an honor to receive each and every story sent to me from the people who enjoy Oshkosh as much as I do. I especially wish to acknowledge the following people:

Lars Hoffman, my husband and best friend, who spent countless hours supporting me with technical issues as well as giving me unshakable emotional support. Thank you for being there.

Tom Poberezny and his staff at EAA for their constant support with helping me get the word out, especially , John Burton, Jack and Golda Cox, Roger Jaynes and Don Purdy. I would also like to send a special thank you to Dick Knapinski for always having answers to my many questions.

Cliff Robertson, Patty Wagstaff, Sean Tucker, Julie Clark, Montaine Mallet, Hoot Gibson, Burt Rutan and Dad, thank you for taking the time out of your busy schedules to share a side of Oshkosh very few of us ever get to see.

Don Alesi, Jim Anderson, Herb Ballou, Al Bartlett, Arlene Beard, Ed Beatty, Harold Bickford, J. Rion Bourgeois, Lynn Butters, Marge Dodge, Claudio Candiota, Ken Cantrell, Dave Gunderson, Geoff Hamence, Michael John Jaeger, John Jenista, Mike McKeig, Chris Miller, David Orr, George Rutan, Irene Rutan, Tonya Rutan, George Savale, Buzz Talbot, Mike Trahan, Ernest Trent, Dean Tresner, Mike Welter, Eric Whittred and Keith Wigglesworth for taking the time to prepare the incredible stories that make up this book.

As always, thank you Mom.

And last I would like to thank all the people of Oshkosh for filling my childhood with wonderful memories.

INTRODUCTION

Every family has stories they love to share when they gather. The EAA member "family" is no different. They reunite each summer in Oshkosh, Wisconsin, home of EAA's National Convention, known as AirVenture Oshkosh. What began in 1953, with Paul Poberezny and a few friends meeting to discuss their airplane designs and love for aviation, has grown into a week long event that draws thousands of people and their airplanes from around the world. Each one of these "family" members has fascinating stories to share of their Oshkosh experiences. I've been fortunate to hear many great stories over the pass twenty years as my father, Voyager Pilot Dick Rutan, took me along each summer to what became our annual "Rutan Family Reunion" at Oshkosh. I thought it might be entertaining to collect some of these stories to share with past, present and future EAA members. Following are some of my favorite Oshkosh stories, submitted to me by attendees.

▼

IT HAPPENED ON THE WAY TO OSHKOSH

▼

Dick Rutan

Voyager—Bound for Oshkosh

I pushed both throttles full forward on the gangly aircraft. The airplane began its takeoff roll down the 10,000 foot runway 30; the longest of the three runways at the Civilian Flight Test Center in Mojave, California.

I say it was a gangly aircraft; it had to be. Its designer, my brother Burt Rutan, had challenged himself to design an aircraft that would circum-navigate the globe non-stop, without refueling, and with a range of 28,000 miles. To accomplish this, extreme compromises had to be made in aircraft stability, controllability, and structural integrity; all of those things that make pilots happy and flying enjoyable. To fly around the world, none of these things could be any part of N269VA, this very unique flying machine we christened VOYAGER.

With no formal funding or sponsorship we scrounged the materials, and the help of dozens of volunteers. With some borrowed, old, worn out Lycoming 0-235 (108HP) engines and some temporary radios, we had an aircraft that would marginally fly. We had convinced ourselves that if we could get this machine flying, the world would see something real and sponsors would flood to our door with their wallets wide open.

That is why on July 27, 1984, we were bound for Oshkosh, Wisconsin, the site of the greatest aviation event in the world. The Voyager had registered only 20 hours of flight test time, having just made its first flight not five weeks before this intended trip. In actuality, Voyager was not anywhere near ready for a long, multi-hour flight away from home, but we needed the funding and felt the experimental airshow at Oshkosh would be the turning point.

With an IFR flight plan on file and Bruce Evans in his VariEze on my wing as safety chase, we rolled down the runway to begin the first of Voyager's many long distance flights.

We had absolutely no idea of the challenges we were about to face on that relatively short flight to Oshkosh. Moments after take off, things began to go awry. We tried to comply with the ATC directions of altitude and airway routing, but had to divert around the monsoonal weather with its connective thunderstorms, scattered rain showers and turbulence. We relied on Bruce as he diverted us around weather, and cleared our changes with ATC, making the workload of flying the airplane teeter on the edge of what I could manage as pilot. This oversized, gangly aircraft, with its temporary engines and systems, needed 110% of my attention. Suddenly there was an acrid, pungent odor of a broken and leaking Hot Stuff glue bottle. The aroma flooded the cockpit. Following that discovery, the auto pilot roll servo (down by my right ankle) had broken it's mounting and was winding its way up my leg, chewing into my pant leg. It's at that very moment I came to the conclusion that we were nowhere near ready to fly to Oshkosh, and as much as I despise the word ABORT, it was obvious that would be our only course of action. I canceled our IFR clearance with Edwards Approach Control and turned back to Mojave bitterly disappointed. This whole trip was going to be much more difficult that I had ever imagined.

After landing safely back in Mojave, we found the mechanical problems were relatively easy to fix. The briefing that followed the landing proved we had learned a lot from this first short 'sojourn' into the world of long distance, cross country flying.

We discovered there was no way the Voyager could punch into the convective clouds and survive the beating. It was obvious we would be forced to fly VFR, and stay clear of the threatening clouds, so we gave up the idea of flying IFR with air traffic control. That decision took a huge workload off of my back. Bruce and I would navigate this trip together, with him flying out ahead to track the clear, smoother air.

Now we had a new, fresh plan. At O' Dark Thirty the next morning, we were ready to takeoff once again and travel to Oshkosh. The flight was progressing well for the first couple of hours, and then we got into Eastern California. This is the height of the summer monsoon season where moisture-laden air is pumped up from Mexico and the gulf. The unstable, moist air mass and the heat from the sun brought constant turbulence as we delicately picked our way through the thunderstorms. We tried to climb above the turbulence level, and that worked for a while, but soon we were high enough to need oxygen. We didn't have any on board, so we couldn't go any higher.

Now trapped in turbulence that was flailing the wings up and down, we were barely able to maintain control as we fought our way across Arizona, New Mexico and then across the Colorado Rockies to the flat plains of eastern Colorado. We lived in constant fear that the next big updraft could pluck the wings off of the airplane. We felt as if we were hanging on to the end of a weakened thread. Bruce would scout ahead for smooth air, but as the day progressed, the sun was heating the fields of the Great Plains, and there was just no smooth air to be found. We just slowly picked our way around, trying to stay out from under the big flat bottom clouds where the strongest updrafts would be. Our flight progress was agonizingly slow to minimize the loads on the structure, and we were seldom over 60 knots indicated; about 20 knots slower than a J-3 Piper Cub flies. By mid afternoon, it was clear there was no way we were going to make Oshkosh before dark and there was no way I was ready to fly this aircraft at night—at least not yet.

Bruce, now tired of making "S" turns to stay with us, pushed it up to find a place we could land and spend the night. Salina, Kansas was selected, and it had big, wide, long runways (it's an ex-Air Force B-52 Base). Beech Aircraft had a manufacturing center there and they welcomed us with a large hangar to bed the Voyager down for the night.

As the time slowly came to begin the descent from 14,000 feet into Salina, we started to get ready for what we knew was going to be the roughest part of the flight. We felt the gusty winds, we saw the dust devils, and we knew it was going to be a major challenge to recover the aircraft in one piece. After 12 hours of intense anguish, I was more than exhausted, and I was physically and mentally drained; yet I knew as we pushed over for the final descent things would get worse. And they got much worse. Jeana unwound the cables for both of the main gear, and I extended the nose gear (the pilot was the only one who could reach the cables underneath of the instrument panel). Memories of being a small child at the swimming pool, climbing up to the high dive platform, looking down and trying to muster the courage to step over the edge to the water below filled my mind and my gut. It took every ounce of will power to reduce both engines to idle and ease the stick forward. My fears of rough air were not unfounded, for the next 40 minutes as we let down the Voyager, we were barely hanging on to the ragged edge of control. I felt the wings go through massive deflections as the up-down drafts of a hot summer night on the Kansas Prairie engulfed the airplane. I didn't have the heart to look and see what was going on with the wings—I just tried to keep the speed under control to minimize the "G" loads. I watched Jeana hold on as best she could without a seat harness or safety belt. I watched the ride slam her hard onto the floor and then fling her up against the ceiling.

Somehow I got the aircraft down on the Salina runway and taxied it into the hangar. I was absolutely spent. How in the world could we ever fly this thing around the world? I couldn't have been more discouraged. I wanted no more of flying, and felt like punching a hole in the fuel tank, setting it on fire using my pilot's license as a wick, and taking a train home. I couldn't imagine ever getting back into that machine and subjecting myself to such anxiety again.

Fortunately, a piece of excellent Kansas beef and a good night's sleep put things in a brighter perspective. We even began to anticipate the welcome we would receive at the greatest airshow on earth when we made it to Oshkosh. Refreshed, we climbed into the airplane, started the engines, taxied out to the runway, and followed Bruce into the early Kansas morning ready to face the 10-hour flight remaining. My recollection of the second leg was not as horrific as the first, but maybe, just maybe, we were getting used to it.

As we got close enough to Oshkosh to make radio contact with the airshow control, we found the airshow underway and officials decided to have the Voyager arrive as the final act of the show for the day. The flight from Salina took only eight hours, but we had to orbit two additional hours before we could land.

Not wanting to detract from the performers before us, we climbed above some puffy clouds and waited. We never did get the autopilot to work, so I had to manually fly the airplane the entire time. The air above Oshkosh, however, was smooth and I could almost relax a little.

Jeana pulled out some powder blue flight suits and wanted us to change into them before landing. I protested and told her there was no way I could get into a flight suit while laying down in an area the size of a bathtub. She put her flight suit on with little trouble, got into the pilot's seat, and took the controls. I slid on my back into the aircraft and attempted to change. It was a major struggle, but much to my surprise, I managed it. In the struggle, I ripped hole in the seam of the crotch and wondered how many of the 1000's we would soon meet would notice.

Soon the airshow below us wound down and it was our turn to descend and land. As we circled down below the clouds, the most amazing spectacle presented itself. The largest crowd I've ever seen in my life were waving handkerchiefs in what looked like a sea of white. They were beckoning us to land, and welcoming Voyager to the airshow. We made it!

Burt was on the public address system describing his aircraft to the enthusiastic crowd. Burt thought the wings flexing was neat and wanted us to demonstrate the wings going up and down. To do this, I had to porpoise the fuselage to make the wings flex. I had just spent the last 22 hours doing my best to stop the flexing, and now Burt wanted to show it off! I very reluctantly complied.

Jeana put the main gear down, I put the nose gear down, and it was finally time to land. Turning right downwind to runway 36, parallel to the handkerchief-waving crowd, I eased the Voyager on to the runway at EAA "Holy Land".

The welcome was tremendous and the dress flight suits (torn crotch and all) looked great. We appeared as fresh and as happy as if we had just arrived first class aboard a B747. Few, if any, would ever know the strain of the past three days efforts.

This would only be a tiny preview to the challenges we would face over the next two and a half years before the world flight and before the Voyager would return once again to Oshkosh. Her final trip to Oshkosh was on the back of a truck en route to the National Air and Space Museum in our nation's capitol where she continues to welcome thousands of visitors daily to the Milestones of Flight Gallery.

I still go to see Voyager. I love to stand in her shadow and listen to moms and dads and grandparents explain to their young ones about the world flight, about achieving the 'impossible', and most important, about believing in dreams.

If you can dream it, you can do it.

*EAA is exporting the freedom and exhilaration of flight to the world.
And with its convention, headquarters and museum being in Oshkosh,
our city is an important partner in that process.
We're glad EAA calls Oshkosh home.*
◆ **Oshkosh (Wis.) Northwestern, July 28, 1998** ◆

▼

Don Alesi

The Great Cross Country Air Race—In a Cessna 140?

Well, we finally made it. Six months of planning finally paid off. Maureen and I, in 1995, completed the race from Jefferson County Airport near Denver, to Oshkosh, Wisconsin. No, we didn't win, but we did finish, and considering we had the smallest, slowest, oldest aircraft, and the youngest pilots with the fewest hours, we did OK.

When preparing for an air race, we needed to do a few things. One was to go on a diet. The other was to call on the experts for some advice. Virginia Rabung raced her Cessna 140 back in the fifties and gave us some much-needed moral support. Nick Selig was there to refresh us on density altitude and to help us with a tail wheel gremlin. The "Blue Skies" pilot shop donated charts, radios and odds and ends.

I thought I'd tell you about some of the lighter moments of the race. Looking back it's easy to laugh at some of our mistakes even though my flight instructor, Dave Morrow, would have pulled his hair out had he been there.

The trip out to Denver took eleven hours of flying. Going around storms was a lot like walking through a cow pasture, being careful where you went or you would be in a pile of stuff.

With a few days to spare before the race started we had time to explore Denver and try to find our way around the one-way streets. After spending a day hiking in Estes Park, our bodies were sore enough so that we actually looked forward to the long flight ahead.

A few words about flight planning. If your hotel does not have the Weather Channel, change hotels. Also lay out the charts and mark your course line at home. The hotel room wasn't long enough and we ended up using the mirrors and pictures on the walls for a straight edge. Someone back home suggested a carpenter's chalk line.

While preparing the 140 on the day before the race, two guys who were also in the race and were checking out the competition approached us. They were racing in a Piper Aerostar and said they had heard about us and wanted to find out if we were crazy. When I told them that we were spending our tenth wedding anniversary flying in the race, they said it was proof enough and continued on their way.

All the other pilots were very friendly and thought it was great we were competing in the race. You would be too if you knew that there was at least one airplane that you could beat. Mooneys, Bonanzas, and Lancairs were the predominating airplanes. The nearest competitors to us were a couple of 172s.

During the pre-race briefing the weather briefer told us about storms in Nebraska that would be dissipating before noon. When I asked how the weather would be later in the afternoon, he seemed confused. Everyone started laughing when he was told we were flying a very slow airplane and a long-term forecast might be necessary.

We were to depart second in the race, which would give us a chance to see a whole lot of passing. Many of the people racing came up to us and wished us luck. One of the organizers asked if we would need anything at the finish line. I suggested rest rooms and possible divorce papers. Fortunately, only one of two items was needed.

Someone told us that we used five thousand feet of runway before the 140 broke ground. Considering how hot it was and the fact that there was nine thousand feet of runway available, I was happy. We would have gone under ground if I could have gotten a weather briefing for it.

During the race, we used 122.75 to communicate with the other pilots. As well as sending back weather information the faster aircraft were asking us if we were okay and promised to save us a hot dog if we could finish. A cold hot dog really makes you want to hurry.

Maureen got her share of IFR work. Every time I changed charts, since space in the 140 is limited, I ended up covering the windshield. I know I should have pre-folded them before we took off.

We stopped in Broken Bow, Nebraska for fuel. After a ten-minute fuel stop, we took off down the four thousand-foot runway without thinking about the heat or density altitude. The 140 used up most of the runway and I had to scoot between some narrow hills just to get some altitude. Maureen thought the engine was shaking when she took the yoke, but the vibration stopped when I let go.

When we called Charles City, Iowa to let them know we were in a race and would like quick service, they had the pumps ready and asked other traffic to let us make a straight-in approach. I think they were shocked and a bit disappointed when we came roaring up in our eighty five-horse monster. Never the less, they did their best and called the traffic to let us out because we needed all the help we could get.

It was 4:00 PM when we departed Charles City. By this time all the other racers were on the ground. At this point, I actually wished we had taken that Alaskan cruise that we had originally planned for our tenth wedding anniversary.

Despite the heat, the weather turned out great. The storms in Nebraska were long gone by the time we went through. As we neared Oshkosh, I began to get over confident and you know what that means.

About ten miles out Maureen called tower. Their first comment was to ask if we were still in the race. A storm was brewing as we began to make our approach into the airport. A shot of turbulence sent the power to idle and we headed away from the storm as Maureen informed that tower that we were heading towards the lake. He offered the approach from there and informed other traffic to give us room.

The rain pelted us as we took our time run down runway 36. The tower then asked us if we could make right traffic for 27. Even though we were at twenty three hundred MSL, Maureen took the yoke put the 140 into a slip that made my fast graying hair stand on end. She put it down right on the numbers and as we taxied up to the ramp, the rain tuned into light drizzle.

As we shut down the engine, a man saw our N number and told us that he soloed our Cessna 140 back in the fifties and was glad to see it still flying.

It was 6:30 PM when we parked and the tower said that our race time was nine hours and ten minutes. With two ten minute fuel stops we were burned out.

The race committee sent a car over to take us to the Theater in the Woods. We had missed only part of the banquet. After the awards fellow racers came over to congratulate us on our last place finish. Apparently, everyone connected with the race had been looking out for us. John and Martha King, from King Videos came over and asked for details on how we flew the race.

A lot of people have asked us if we would do it again. So far, we are saying "no way", but looking back, I can see how people like Virginia Rabung did it more than once. I think everyone should try an air race to Oshkosh. It's like one cross-country after another. Only you are doing it with a bunch of people.

The next time somebody or some group tells me aviation, as we know it is going to end if this or that a new rule is enacted, I'm going to try to remember Oshkosh and the EAA, with its tangible proof that the regulated and the regulators can work together.
◆ J. Mac McClellan, FLYING magazine, Oct. 1997 ◆

▼

Dean Tresner

Mugged in Chicago

I flew my Kitfox from New York to Oshkosh (my third time) this year and, as usual, I planned the flight to spend the previous weekend in Chicago. That way, if the weather got bad over Pennsylvania (as it often does) I could still make the show on time.

Well, the weather was good this year and I hit the Windy City on Saturday night. I was planning to spend the next three nights on the waterfront and then continue on.

Late on Sunday night, I was walking back to the hotel when a mugger snuck up behind me with a blunt object. He hit me in the back of the head and, again, in the face. I remember my head hitting the sidewalk with a thump! I was out for only a second and then I shoved him off of me before he could get my wallet. We both ran off in different directions.

After I got back from the hospital (with twenty stitches) I remember laying in bed thinking: 'Damn, he took Oshkosh from me.'

The staff at the hotel was very understanding and I was told that, despite the fact that they were sold out for the week, I could stay as long as I needed to.

After four days of television and room service, I felt the concussion had subsided enough and I was airworthy again. I checked out and went back to Meigs where I found a gray scum covering all of the windward surfaces of my aeroplane (I guess she didn't have a very good time in Chicago either.)

I got to Oshkosh and, after some shenanigans in the pattern (I HAD been hit in the head,) I parked with the other Kitfoxes.

The show wasn't as exciting to me as those of years past, partly, I'm sure, because I didn't feel like walking around much. But I set up my chair under the wing and answered people's questions. Especially those questions from the kids. They love my aeroplane. (Mainly, they tell me, because it looks like a watermelon.) Promoting our special love of flight among the young has turned out to be one of the best (and unexpected) things about being in this game.

My most stressful moment of the whole trip, oddly, turned out to be during the Skystar dinner; attended by what must have been at least two hundred people. At one point, during the President's remarks, he asked those of us who flew our own planes to the airshow to stand up. Well and good, I was in the very back. But then he asked all of us to step up to the mike and say a few words about our trip.

Now, having a black eye is embarrassing enough, but in front of all those people! I was mortified. Timidly, I said it was a good flight, except for the mugging, and then tried to slink off the stage. He took the mike back and said, "Wait a minute, what was that last thing?"

I had to go back and explain. So I did. And a strange thing happened; as I talked about my experience, I gained more confidence and, at the end, with hardly a trace of self-consciousness, I said: "I'm just glad to be here."

I sure was.

It's all pretty heady stuff, and there's more stuff at Oshkosh each summer than anywhere else in the world of homebuilt aircraft.
◆ **Dave Martin, KITPLANES, Nov. 1997** ◆

▼

Claudio Candiota

From Brazil to Oshkosh

I fell in love with airplanes very early. Maybe even before I was born. My father was a pilot, loved airplanes and took part in 1940 (11 years before I was born) on a countrywide campaign which the aim was to provide Brazilian Flight Schools and Airclubs with single engine training airplanes. My parent's godfather in their wedding was a very important person in the Brazilian Aviation History. His name was Joaquim Pedro Salgado Filho. He was the first Minister of Aeronautics of Brazil.

My mother almost gave birth on board of a DC-3 in 1951. I was born minutes after the airplane landed. Two months later, I was back on board of another DC-3. Believe me or not, my mother kept the ticket. My first airplane ticket issued in 1951. I still have it in my files. The ticket is so old that Varig (Brazilian Airlines) wants me to donate it for its Aviation Museum.

My uncle (my father's brother) is also an Aviation Pioneer. His name is Clovis Candiota. He was the first agricultural pilot of Brazil. He made his first crop dusting flight in August 19, 1947, in the City of Pelotas, State of Rio Grande do Sul, and the southernmost state of Brazil. August 19th is now recognized by the Institute of Brazilian Aeronautical History as the Brazilian Agricultural Aviation National Day. I guess you could say I was born with AVGAS in my blood.

The first time I heard about Oshkosh was in the early 1980's. I have always traveled a lot throughout the States because I own a travel agency. Besides that, since a young student, I have worked with international cultural exchange programs. These jobs made me travel a lot, meeting people and learning about the American Culture.

I never flew my own airplane to Oshkosh. I always flew commercial. The first time I went by myself. The second time I took a few friends along with me. I kept returning, year after year, with more and more people. Growing numbers to the point we gathered 280 pilots to travel with me, in 1997. This was the largest group flying together present at the Convention that year.

It is a little different from people who fly in their small airplanes to Oshkosh, but not less challenging. In order to put this group together, we must work with a lot of planning and logistics. We advertise with more than one year in advance and everything must be booked, paid and confirmed before we even start advertising.

Even though we have people staying at the Park Plaza Hotel in downtown Oshkosh, it is at South Scott Hall, at UWO, where most pilots like to stay. In order to compensate the lack of air conditioning, we keep an storage room, full of fans, all year round to hand one to each passenger when they arrive. We have meetings and parties almost every night, to keep the spirit of aviation alive. We talk about what we saw during the day at the show, while having a few beers. A typical daily pilots chat to exchange ideas. After so many years, a group of Americans began to stay with us. This American group is also growing every year. They call us from the States to make sure they will get a room in the same building and the same floors were we, the Brazilians, will stay. We made a lot of friends after almost 20 years attending the EAA Convention.

We made friends among Brazilians, among Americans and among people from all over the world. Among Brazilians because they come from each and every state of Brazil. Some fly over 30 hours from their hometowns to Oshkosh.

Although you may think we don't encounter challenges when flying airliners, try to fly from Brazil to Oshkosh with 280 pilots and aviation enthusiasts, of all ages, in two different airplanes, connecting with two others in Miami, heading to Chicago to load a bunch of buses to get to Oshkosh. All the guests are all crazy about airplanes, most do not speak English and you are being asked questions almost twenty-four hours a day, for seven days. Believe me: it is a true challenge. We have people coming from all over the country, from the Amazon to even neighboring countries such as Uruguay and Argentina. Families with kids, sometimes three generations of pilots traveling together. We have pilots who flew with us more than 15 times, like the pilot called José Selomar Oliveira. A governor, a senator, Air Force Officials, you name it, if you're from Brazil and love airplanes, then you want to go to Oshkosh with us.

We even sponsored a crazy friend who was the first pilot to fly a Motorglider from Porto Alegre, Brazil to Oshkosh. His name was Jose Alberto Carvalho. He took-off his PT-PME (N Number), on July 9, 1990 and flew 17000 kilometers (10 thousand some miles). The trip took 13 days and 86 flight hours. Carvalho died on Feb 29, 1992 when he crashed his Glasair III, doing aerobatics at low altitude over an airfield nearby. He was one of our every year participants. We miss him a lot. He made history in Brazil with this flight to Oshkosh and with another one, when he crossed the Andes Mountains flying the same motorglider. Now, just imagine how crazy he was. Flying a slow-single-engine-all-white-motorglider over the all white Andes Mountains in Chile. If he crashed, he would have never been found. We still miss him a lot and will miss him forever.

How do we overcome such challenges? With a lot of patience and love for airplanes, of course, but much more than that, with love for the people, for getting together, for meeting these friends once again. Hoping next year, we will be blessed and have our way crossed by another nice person from some country somewhere in the world with whom we at least have this love in common: love for aviation.

▼

David Orr

Glass Overcast

It sometimes looks so effortless with the planes flying over in formations, but there is a lot of talent displayed in the old warbird flyovers. I've flown formations since 1969 and it comes easy in a two or three ship; but flyovers of dozens is very different.

Norm Howell and I met with civilian pilots one Saturday a month every month for most of the first half of 1995 and were quite happy to organize and encourage 18 Long-EZ drivers from California in making the short trip to Oshkosh to participate in "Glass Overcast '95". We were told that leading homebuilders in formation was like herding cats. True at first, we were heartened as first one and another became almost military in their precision and discipline. We got to Oshkosh as part of a bigger sixty-seven-plane line of EZs, which arrived like cats after a ball of yarn. We had visions of little herds of Long-EZ's heading off in who knows what direction, but nevertheless, come "show day", the gaggle of twenty-eight planes lifted off and were actually into formation within a 270 degree turn out! We had such a ball that we have been trying to figure out when to do it again. The Long-EZ is so much like a fighter plane for formation practice and simple fear of looking unmilitary probably kept the cats in order, at least until the turn to downwind where one decided on a barrel roll in the pattern. Thank goodness for invisibility in these wondrous homebuilts.

▼

JUST BEING THERE

Oshkosh represents something very special,
a uniquely American celebration.
◆ **Former President George Bush** ◆

▼

Buzz Talbot

"Why You Come Here?"

"Excuse me...excuse me...pardon me."

I looked up, realizing the foreign sounding tongue was being directed at me as opposed to the tens of thousands of people surrounding me and my Long-EZ N112TG on row 34 at Oshkosh.

"Why you come here?"

"What?" I didn't understand what the dark-skinned man with the neatly rolled turban on his head meant.

"Why you come here?" he repeated, sweeping one arm gesturing to the rows of shark fins that could only be Rutan designs.

Why did I come here for the past seven years in a row? I hate the pressing crowds that often abuse the plane. I hate the over priced greasy food. I hate the port-a-potties. I hate parking my car a mile away from my plane and paying each day for the privilege. I really hate the show biplane Samson, which is almost as loud as the AV8 Harrier jump jet. So why do I come here year after year?

"I think...to see my friends again. This is the only place where all of us meet. This man next to me flew all the way from Brazil to be with his fellow builders" I replied, hoping that Andre Deberdt's 5,000 mile adventure in his Long-EZ PP-ZAD would interest the visitor but his gaze did not waver.

"They pay you come here? How much they pay you come here?" the man in the turban wasn't buying the friendship motive, but what a wild idea! EAA paying homebuilders to display the results of our years of toil! I smiled as I thought of $100 paid to each of the nearly three thousand homebuilt/show planes at Wittman Field.

"No, they don't pay me anything" I replied slowly, so he would understand.

"They no pay you come here?" the man asked more confused than ever.

Maybe a personal explanation would help. I pointed to my white flight line pass, riveted about my wrist, as I noticed the man in the turban also had a weekly pass on his wrist.

"You paid to come here, right?" I asked as I now pointed at his wrist-band. The white turban began to nod up and down.

"I paid to come here too, just like you." I explained. The dark brown eyes under the turban grew large with disbelief.

"You pay come here? You pay? Why you pay come here?" The visitor from the East pleaded for enlightenment.

"We all pay to come here." I answered with a pointing finger to the thousands of homebuilt planes stretched as far as the eye could see.

The man in the turban called over to a very beautiful woman in a sari dress holding a small child. "Excuse me. I take picture of child in plane?" he asked humbly.

As I lifted the little girl in the crisply starched white dress into the front seat of my plane I felt like a celebrity. The man in the turban probably just wanted photographic proof that UFO's really do exist and that the aliens are willing to pay to be put on public display.

Once inside the alien craft the little girl, who looked more like a stiff doll than a real little girl, began to loudly cry in pleading protest. She didn't want to be whisked away by the alien in his strange craft.

I motioned to the mother to put her arm around her daughter so the man in the turban could take his picture. She too seemed a little fearful of the plane but went to the rescue of her daughter. With the mother holding her and forcing a smile, the man in the turban snapped his picture, and then another just to be sure.

I lifted the little doll out of the front cockpit and she ran to the man in the turban. He bowed and turned and walked away, the woman in the sari a very respectful 10 paces to his rear.

I don't know if he ever got the answer to the persistent question, "Why you come here?"

Maybe the answer cannot be analyzed from so many words into a rational explanation.

Maybe why we come to Oshkosh once a year is more feeling than thought.

For some, like Andre Deberdt's 5,000 mile trek from Brazil in his Long-EZ, the reason for coming to Oshkosh is similar to the reason why we climb Mt. Everest. Some have lost their lives flying to Oshkosh despite the best plans and intentions. Weather and fate can be just as cruel a hunter en route to Oshkosh as up the face of Everest.

I know of an EAA member who had volunteered to help out at Oshkosh for many years. After learning he had cancer and had only months to live, he returned to Oshkosh to volunteer for the last time. How do you rationally explain that in mere words?

Many have said coming to Oshkosh is like coming home to your long lost hometown during the county fair. Sure the championship hog smells, and it's too hot and the ice-cold lemonade is watered down and the hotdogs are over priced, but it's home. You can just feel that it's right. It's why we come here.

It's a wonderful show.
It's hard to get a sense of how many folks are involved
in this sort of aviation from where I live on the East Coast.
It's a wonderful display of enthusiasm,
professionalism and proficiency in aviation.
◆ **John F. Kennedy Jr.** ◆

▼

Jill Rutan Hoffman
My Autograph

I will never forget the Oshkosh when someone asked me for my autograph. I think of it as my moment of appreciation. I was used to admirers asking Dad and Jeana for an autograph, but never my own. And it happened in the most unexpected way.

It was the Oshkosh following Dad and Jeana's historic world flight and they were the most popular couple on the flight line. The pair would sit for hours signing autograph books, posters and even T-shirts while I sat and waited. Dad's favorite thing was to torment any child who asked for his autograph. He believed that the poor kid was forced into the request by his parents. "Do you know who I am?" Dad would ask. Once or twice the response was "Chuck Yeager". This always made Dad laugh and he never sent anyone back empty-handed.

My moment of appreciation came while the whole group was out enjoying a meal at one of Oshkosh's fine restaurants. I was sitting there with Dad on one side and Jeana on the other, when I noticed a group at a table near us was pointing our way. Then suddenly a man got up from his seat and came directly over to give me his autograph book for my signature. Not Dad's and not Jeana's but mine. I acted as if I were an old pro and signed it "Best Wishes, Jill Rutan" and handed it back to my admirer. I was a little embarrassed because I noticed my hands were shaking but I went on with dinner as if nothing happened. I did notice that when the man returned to his group they all examined my signature closely. Then another member of the group got up, and once again, came to our table. I naturally thought that I was going to be interrupted again so I put down my fork only to see him walk right pass me to Jeana. While Jeana was signing her name I noticed that my name had been scratched out. At that moment it became clear to me that I had just been mistaken for Jeana Yeager.

Looking back on this I still laugh realizing how easy it is to get caught up in the moment. I was humbled from that experience and realized that I have always been appreciated. But even more, I'm fortunate to have had the opportunity to be Dick Rutan's daughter at Oshkosh.

It was an outstanding event because of the number of airplanes safely flown in for the event. It was tremendous because of the enormous variety of airplanes that managed to be parked on the flight line. The fly-in was enjoyed again this year because of all the volunteers who turned out to make it happen. The EAA Fly-In is much more than a great airshow every afternoon. It's a great deal more than a 'family' gathering of aviation enthusiasts. This great aviation extravaganza has become the heart and soul of aviation!

◆ **General Aviation News and Flyer, Aug. 1997** ◆

▼

Ed Beatty

Tales of Emotion, Devotion, Honesty and Integrity

Stan Gomoll is a pleasant man who owns an airplane very near and dear to my heart, a Waco EQC-6 and it's been to Oshkosh every year that I've been there. Stan doesn't fly anymore, due to a health problem, but now his son flies the plane down from Minneapolis with Stan in the right seat. The reason the plane is special to me is that it's just like the one I had my first airplane ride in, 1939. I was eleven years old and the plane was three. For the pass fifteen years I've spent time walking around this plane, admiring it, petting it and wishing I could take her around the field a couple of times. Then at last in 1989 I had my picture taken standing in front of it fifty years to the month that I took that first adventure into the blue. Only at Oshkosh can you relive some of your fondest memories.

*   *   *   *

Oshkosh is loaded with merchants, many of which are hawking their wares to promote their primary interest in aviation. One of these organizations is the "Save a Connie Foundation" (SAC). This group of people is composed of persons enthralled with the Lockheed Constellation—a plane used by many of the major airlines in the 50's and 60's prior to the introduction of jetliners. The Air Force and Navy used them well into the late 70's and they were designated the C-121. I spent twenty-six hours on one of them on the way to France in 1961 and then made a round trip to Puerto Rico in 1970 aboard one of them operated by the Pennsylvania Air National Guard. It was a great plane and the SAC has done a fine job in restoring their plane to flying condition.

I was standing in their booth examining the items they were selling to raise money. They had the usual ball caps, T-shirts, pictures, coffee mugs, pins etc. Most were slightly overpriced but it was for a good cause—I bought a cap. As I stood there a man and his little boy, perhaps four years old stood near me. The little boy was obviously excited by all that was around him. Among the items he saw were some little plastic wings. He wanted to buy them and his father said "no". A man turned to the father and said "Do you mind if I gave you son the wings?" The father agreed it would be all right and the man handed the clerk fifty cents. He then pinned the wings on the little boy's shirt. "There" he said, "now you look like the rest of us pilots." The little boy's eyes glistened with delight and his smile was from ear to ear. "What do you say?" the father asked. "Sunk you sir," the little boy mumbled. "My pleasure," the man replied. "Keep em' flying son!" Then he turned and strode away with his head high and shoulders back and a look of pleasure on his face. This is Oshkosh!

*   *   *   *

Two small boys were walking our way coming from the grocery store, which is directly across the street from where I camp each year. They were perhaps nine and twelve years old respectively and as they approached us the younger boy tossed a candy wrapper on the ground. The paper had barely touched the grass when the older boy quickly admonished his younger friend "Pick that up!" he said, "and put it in the waste can over there. This is Oshkosh and we don't throw things on the ground around here." Wouldn't it be wonderful if the entire world was an Oshkosh?

*   *   *   *

I was walking through the crowd on the flight line following one of the tractor drawn trams full of airshow visitors, when something dropped to the pavement. A young man stooped down quickly and picked it up and then ran after the tram. He handed the item to the narrator sitting at the back. "Has anyone lost their weekly pass badge?" the narrator asked over the speaker system. Sure enough a passenger held up his hand. A weekly pass is worth a lot of money and if you lose it you buy another one. That young man deserved a thank you if not a reward. By the time it was returned to the owner he was long gone, swallowed in a sea of humanity and content with the knowledge he had been of service to someone and happy with his honesty. Oshkosh reminds you that the good basic values such as trust and honesty have not disappeared.

*   *   *   *

The **Kids from Wisconsin** are one of the finest groups of musicians to be seen anywhere. They are hand picked for their talents and range in age from sixteen through nineteen. They can be a member of the group for no more than four years and cannot stay past their twentieth birthday. Most of them are multi-talented singing, dancing, and instrumental, many playing more than one instrument. These "kids" usually kick off the Convention each year with their first night performance at The Theater in the Woods. This is an open-air theater built in a park area near the flight line where all the evening programs are held. When the "kids" perform it's standing room only. One year we sat in rain coats under umbrellas to watch their show and enjoyed every minute of it. Ultimately, the rain shedding from our umbrellas poured down the collars of our raincoats. It is amazing how normally uncomfortable situations become treasured memories at Oshkosh.

*   *   *   *

Nearly five thousand volunteers make Oshkosh work and being a part of the volunteer program makes it all seem more worthwhile. Our friends from Tomah, the Bradys, spend countless hours working in camp registration. John Brady is a cap collector. When he wears his blue hat he is working in camper registration, a yellow hat he is working for security and the red one is his chapter hat. John also has a white hat he wears when playing host to the PROTECT PT-1 builders group which assembles each year to discuss building and flying. In addition to all of this John helps out with Operation Thirst, but they don't give out hats for that. The countless hours volunteers spend at Oshkosh is what makes this fly-in grand.

*   *   *   *

Everyone should try Oshkosh at least once. Even if you have no interest in aviation the people make it interesting. It is a totally different atmosphere from most other outdoor events. It's cleaner and a little nosier at times (unless you count the cheering crowds at ball games), but it's far different from a fair because there are no rides, except in the airplanes of course. There are so many things that happen in the two weeks that one story can't cover them. See you at Oshkosh!

It's a remarkable experience. Respect—that's the word I use
for the people who attend.
◆ **former "Good Morning America" host David Hartman** ◆

▼

George Savale

The Volmer Amphibian Project

I started hanging around the local airport in New Jersey in 1939-40 and bumming rides whenever possible. Some resulted in some right seat time, which I enjoyed very much. When I returned after WWII in 1946, I went to work as an insurance adjuster to follow my father's footsteps. Several transfers later I opened the "New" office in Glens Falls, NY and with my friend Sam Greenawait, (A former Army AF instructor) adjusted several aircraft claims, and made some repairs, especially on the old tube type radios, which required test flights to make sure the repairs were right. I was also sent on some "Storm" expeditions, following hurricane catastrophes, where I was able to fly at company expense. After leaving the adjusting field full time, in 1959, I could no longer fly because I couldn't afford it.

After my first wife passed away, I remarried, despite being almost bankrupt from medical and bad debt expenses, and although I read aviation magazines occasionally, it seemed just a daydream to fly again, until in 1991 a friend told me about a Volmer amphibian project that was for sale. I bought the project, which was a partial fuselage, one partial wing, and a lot of pieces. (No avionics, no engine, no wheels, ect.) By 1994 I had redesigned the plans to fit my ideas of what a good low and slow amphib should be, but without any enthusiasm on my wife's part. (She had never flown in a light plane.)

I had recently completed my second camper van, after 145,000 miles on the first one, and we decided to take a trip to Alaska. We left our home in St. Petersburg FL about April 26th and then went to our NY camp and project place outside of Glens Falls. About May 20th we headed out to the Ford Museum and then, via the Upper Peninsula, to Montana. We took the Alcan Highway to Fairbanks, toured Alaska from Chicken (26 nice people and 1 old grouch!) to Valdeez and then south to Vancouver and from there to Tucson AZ. We went back though Denver and somehow arrived at Oshkosh about 3 weeks before the convention.

I told my wife I needed to do some research on my project, and was fortunate enough to meet Ben Owen. He not only gave me more information than I intended to get, but talked my wife into staying on and volunteering in the library, even though she really wanted to go home after living for 9 weeks in a van. We stayed, and she made so many friends, (some Sun 'n Fun volunteers too) that she has been anxious to return almost every year since.

I was also fortunate enough to be able to fly a Volmer plus meet with Volmer Jenssen, while out there. (Volmer gave my project his blessing, but said I shouldn't call it a Volmer because it was so different from his design.) We are presently at Sun 'n Fun volunteering, and will be working at Oshkosh selling memberships at the main gate. I'll never regret the day I found that Volmer Amphibian project because it helped my wife and I discover a new way of life that only Oshkosh can deliver.

During the rest of the year, we may be frustrated, beaten-down and disgusted by the whole system, but Oshkosh will revive us. Certain interests tell us general aviation is dying; Oshkosh proves they are wrong. FAA Washington promises us user fees, tighter regulation, less service and more hassle. Oshkosh empowers us to cope with these tactics and fight back. About the time we think we're the only ones left, we gather under a wing with some kindred spirits and find out we're not.
◆ **Leroy Cook, Private Pilot, Nov. 1997** ◆

▼

Mike Trahan

Oshkosh at Long Last

One of the first things I heard after becoming a pilot was "Man, you have to go to Oshkosh!" I soon learned that Oshkosh meant the EAA Annual Convention and Fly-In at Oshkosh, Wisconsin. Many of my flying friends had been and all came back with glowing accounts of their experiences there. The trip to Oshkosh has become an annual ritual for them. It is their "pilgrimage" to "Aviation Mecca".

Going to Oshkosh was something I always wanted to do, but since it took me four decades to get there, I suppose it was one of those things that had to happen when the time was right. 1999 was the year we finally made it.

My wife Sheila and our son Jim went with me. Jim started flying a few months before our trip to Wisconsin. I thought it was ironic that it took me so long to get there, and there was Jim, the brand new pilot, attending the same show. I would not have had it any other way.

Lodging was not a problem for us. Sheila has relatives in Appleton, which is twenty miles from Oshkosh. Years ago her Aunt Pat gave us a standing invitation to come visit, enjoy free room and board, and go to Oshkosh. It took us two days to drive from Texas to Appleton. We arrived at Aunt Pat's on a Friday evening. At six thirty the next morning we were standing at the EAA AirVenture entrance gate.

We walked under the big Welcome sign and into the exhibit area. The first thing to grab our attention was the British Airways Concorde. It was the centerpiece of a dazzling array of display aircraft. I looked around and all I could see were beautiful airplanes everywhere. That moment can only be described as a near religious experience for me.

We had no map of the field but we knew that anything we ran across would be great. We picked a random direction and headed out. In a few minutes we found ourselves in the Classic Aircraft tie down area. The sun was just beginning to appear on the horizon and everything felt soft and still. It was so peaceful. There were a few people walking around and admiring the flawless airplanes on display. They spoke in hushed tones and moved slowly. I think they knew they were in a very special place. It reminded me of the time I visited some ancient cathedrals in Europe and the way people reacted to those places. Everyone treated this area with the same reverence and respect.

We talked with some of the pilots who were camping under the wings of their airplanes. They were having their first cup of coffee of the day, and they swelled with pride when we showed an interest in their restoration handiwork. This was the perfect place to start our day at Oshkosh.

At seven thirty airplanes from all over the field started taxiing toward the runway. It was the morning ritual. Some were off for their hundred-dollar breakfast, others just going out for a showoff flight, and still others were taking kids flying as part of the EAA Young Eagles project. We went to the end of a row of airplanes, stopped as close as possible to the active taxiway, and watched the parade. It seemed endless. I recognized some of the planes, didn't recognize most of them, and lusted after them all. It was almost too much. Now I know the true meaning of the word sensory overload.

The rest of the morning was spent visiting as many exhibits, vendor booths, and aircraft displays as possible. Then it was time for the airshow to begin. We found a good vantage point near the show plane ramp and settled in. Visiting with the people around us filled some of the waiting time. Airplane people are always interesting. A man standing nearest to us had a hand held VHF receiver. He was happy to let us enjoy the two-way chatter between the tower and the airplanes with him. After a short wait the show started.

The first treat was the takeoff of the Concorde SST. British Airways was offering a supersonic flight from Oshkosh into Canada and back for anyone who could come up with the price of admission. It was expensive, but all four flights that weekend were full.

A security guard turned to the crowd as the Concorde taxied into position for takeoff. He warned, "Be sure to cover your ears when he starts to power up. The decibels that thing puts out, even at this distance, can do permanent damage to your hearing." We believed him and did what he said. When that airplane's afterburners lit you could literally feel the power reverberating in your bones. I thought about the times I stood near the runway at Webb AFB, feeling that same sensation, as the T-38's, with their burners ablaze, flashed by me on takeoff roll.

I am not a great airshow fan, but this was one of the best I have ever seen. I even took personal interest in a couple of the acts. The first was the Budweiser BD-5 Jet. One of the BD-5 airshow pilots is Bill "Burner" Beardsly. Bill and I met when he reported for Delta's Flight Engineer simulator training. I was one of his instructors. Bill is a former member of the Navy Blue Angels, a very unassuming man considering all he has accomplished, and an outstanding pilot. My only disappointment was that I could not get close enough to him to say hello.

The other act was Chuck Yeager and Bud Anderson flying two P-51 Mustangs. Chuck and Bud were combat wing mates in WWII. It's still difficult to believe that we were actually watching two seventy plus year old men flying fifty six year old airplanes. It was almost like seeing Babe Ruth hitting a home run or Ben Hogan getting a hole in one. The big difference is that Babe and Ben did their thing long ago. Chuck and Bud are still doing it!

I believe Ed and Connie Bolin own both of the Mustangs. They were painted in the same colors that were used by Chuck and Bud during the war. Ed is a retired Delta Captain and Connie is one of our active pilots. I met her when she was still a flight attendant. Now she is a Captain on the Boeing 767. She has come a long way baby. After Bud and Chuck finished their flight, Connie hopped into "Glamorous Glen III" and took off to join the other Mustangs in the holding pattern. She was part of the warbird finale.

By the time the airshow ended we were hurting all over. Our feet were killing us and we wanted to go home. We had been there nearly twelve hours. However, there was one more thing we wanted to do, and that was attend mass there at Oshkosh. We walked over to the Theater in the Woods just in time to find a seat before services started. There were at least a thousand people there. I didn't recognize any of them, but I'll bet many of them are in the who's who of aviation. Guess where that theater was. It was right next to the Classic Aircraft line! We had come full circle.

We went back to Aunt Pat's that night, completely overwhelmed by what we had seen. Sheila decided to visit family the next day rather than return with us. Jim and I were at the gate at six o'clock this time. We spent a lot of time visiting the exhibit halls, trying out headsets, and comparing the GPS systems that were offered. It amazed me how much general aviation navigation has changed since the last time I was involved in it. Some of the systems were as good as or even better than those I use on the airliners I fly.

Oshkosh doesn't wait around. It gets to you right away. Go there once and you will be hooked for life. Jim and I had seen enough for this time, but we vowed that we would be back next year, and the next, and the next.

The people with EAA, who produce this show, are the best at what they do. There is no gathering in the aviation world quite like Oshkosh.

Now I know why so many people return to Oshkosh year after year. It is not just an airshow it is their annual trip to "Aviation Mecca"! People come to celebrate their love of flying. I know that was why I was there, and I have never felt a closer kinship.

Oshkosh is becoming an aviation institution, providing something for everyone. Without a doubt, it rates top billing on the list of 'must dos' for aviation enthusiasts the world over.
◆ **World Engineering magazine, Sept./Oct. 1996** ◆

▼

Marge Dodge

Welcome To Oshkosh!

My romance with flying began as a romance with a man. It was a warm, clear California winter day when we took off in a rental Cessna over San Diego Bay and headed along the coast viewing La Jolla, Del Mar, and points north. In 1970 the skies and the coastline were still fairly pristine and unspoiled and the clear day only added to the romance of seeing the world from a whole new perspective. The romance evolved to include marriage and a dream to build an airplane. Over the years the dream persisted, until it was realized with the completion of our Long-EZ in 1994.

After many years of fueling the dream with EAA membership and faithfully reading Sport Aviation, we began building the Long-EZ in the basement of a log cabin in the isolated mountains of New Mexico. During the almost three years of construction, I was busy with my professional career and was only able to assist in a limited capacity with the "two man" jobs and in the "unskilled labor" department. I was able to offer support when certain tasks appeared to be daunting, like wiring the instrument panel. My husband/builder had never faced such a project and was somewhat discouraged, when I pointed out to him that building an airplane is not unlike running a marathon race. When a marathon runner "hits the wall" at mile 20, he can't just stop, because he has come so far and has just a little bit further to go. Building an airplane is just like that, you have to focus on how much you have accomplished, not how much more there is to do and just like the runner, when he hurts the most and wants to quit the most, that is the time to dig just a little deeper and finish the race.

Finish is just what we did with the final FAA certification and the maiden voyage on a mountain runway at 9,000-ft. Elevation in 1994. During that year we flew our airplane to a variety of airshows and events and a whole new world unfolded before us as never anticipated. When the dream of building our own airplane began, we never anticipated the freedom of flying, the wonderful experiences we would have, nor the interesting people we would meet. At each event I would see a new airplane I had never seen before, meet exciting people from all walks of life that shared the common bond of sport aviation, and hear stories that filled me with awe. I learned aviation is much more than just flying, it is the constant process of learning and sharing.

In 1995 we knew we were ready to fly the Long-EZ to Oshkosh. Several weeks prior to the flight, we packed our bags (our very small bags), and studied all the special arrival and departure procedures until we were ready to "rock our wings". Our early morning departure under blue Southwestern skies was as uneventful as our one stop flight to Oshkosh. The realization that we had finally completed our dream and were actually flying to Oshkosh began to materialize over the railroad tracks near Fond du Lac and our excitement increased as we were identified by the tower as "white and blue EZ". We rocked our wings and landed smoothly on runway 36, taxied over to the home built show plane parking, lowered our nose, and cut the engine. As we opened the canopy, the young Civil Air Patrol that guided us to our parking place said, "Welcome to Oshkosh!". My ears heard those three words, but my heart heard, "Congratulations, you had a dream and the commitment and dedication to accomplish that dream, and I salute you and all of those who showed you the way, and all of those you will inspire in the future." For that is what Oshkosh means to me, the coming together of wonderful, talented people whom all have a dream and the dedication to achieve that dream, not only to achieve unbelievable success, but to inspire greatness in others.

So each year since, we have returned for the Oshkosh experience and to hear those three words, "Welcome to Oshkosh!"

▼

THERE I WAS

When I come to Oshkosh, I meet people who are on the frontier. The first 'a' in NASA is 'Aeronautics.' Our customer base is here and we have to make sure our vision for the future of aviation in America meets up with expectations these folks have. We get our report card, in a way, here at Oshkosh.
◆ **NASA Administrator Dan Goldin, July 1998** ◆

▼

Robert "Hoot" Gibson

Mig Pilot

I first attended the Experimental Aircraft Association (EAA) Annual Convention at Oshkosh in 1985. I had been a member of EAA since 1983 when I started rebuilding a homebuilt airplane, a Cassutt, but I had been aware of Oshkosh since as far back as I can remember. 1985 was the first year I actually made it there, and I flew a NASA T-38 in with fellow Astronaut Bob Overmyer. He and I had been selected to attend by NASA because EAA had asked for a couple of Astronauts who were fans of home-built experimental airplanes and EAA members. Bob had a two-seat "Starduster" biplane that he had owned for years in Houston, and it was a regular sight over the NASA Space Center. This was Bob's first year to attend as well, and he flew the T-38 from Houston to Scott Air Force Base with me in the back seat and we refueled for the leg in to Oshkosh. I had the thrill of flying the front seat into Wittman Field at Oshkosh, and it was indeed a real thrill and a real eye-opener! We arrived on an IFR flight plan, and once we switched over to Tower, the fun really started. The frequency was so congested that I couldn't get a word in to announce to Tower that we were there, and I was worried a bit about how this was all going to work. We were short on fuel to go anywhere else, and it was impossible to cut in on the talk on the Tower frequency. Tower knew right where we were though, and in the midst of all the chaos came up and said "NASA, what is your distance from the field?" When I replied "7 miles", he told me to call 4 miles out. That happened fairly quickly because even with gear and flaps down, we were still travelling at 170 knots. When I called 4 miles, Tower said "OK, all traffic on final to runway 26, climb to 1500 feet and go around". I have to admit, I felt very bad about the disruption to the pattern, but I was really happy to be safely on the ground. We still had to work our way across the field through all the traffic on the ground, and it was about 30 minutes before we were spotted in our parking spot and could shut down the left engine. I had shut down the right engine as soon as we were off the runway because I could see it was going to take a while to get through all the traffic, and I was worried we might run out of fuel taxiing!

Bob Overmyer and I had a very busy time at Oshkosh that year because the day we arrived, the Space Shuttle "Challenger" launched and suffered an engine failure during launch, the only engine failure ever in the Space program. The local Press was extremely interested in the story (as were we!), and Bob and I spent a considerable amount of time on the phones back to Houston to get the facts of the incident so we could brief the Press and the attendees at the Convention. The Space Shuttle was able to make it to a safe orbit in a sequence of events we called "Abort to Orbit", or ATO. The orbit was raised somewhat higher after extensive calculations by Mission Control on the amount of fuel reserve and the "Challenger" was able to fly a completely successful mission. It certainly made 1985 a most memorable year for me to make my first trip to Oshkosh! I failed to make it back the next year, 1986, because of the loss of the "Challenger" in January of that year, but I have made it every other year since then. Sadly, Bob Overmyer was killed in 1996 while flight testing an experimental aircraft prototype.

I became involved in a flying museum in Houston that was founded by a good friend named Jim Robinson. I had first met Jim at a local airport,

Clover Field in Friendswood, where I kept my homebuilt "Cassutt". He had a Pitts Special at the time and we had a great many good times in the flying fraternity at Clover Field and at Jim's ranch and airfield near Pleasonton Texas. Jim started flying jet fighters in about 1986 when he acquired a T-33 and started flying airshows in the airplane. The love of jets is infectious, and before you knew it, Jim had an F-86 and a Mig-15, and would acquire still more. I was always a fan of the F-86, but I was absolutely fanatical to fly that Mig! I bothered Jim relentlessly for the next couple years and he finally agreed to bring me onboard as a "Mig pilot" in 1988. He was expanding the museum which had the name "Combat Jets Flying Museum", and it was intended to be a flying monument to the first generation of jet fighters. Eventually it would include no less than 9 jet fighters. I was always very grateful to Jim for letting me be part of this exciting group. We made it to countless airshows for years, including of course, Oshkosh. In 1988 and 1989, I flew the Mig-15 to Oshkosh, and we flew all our airplanes in the show there, including a mock Korean War dogfight between the F-86 and the Mig-15. I was always the loser, since the Mig had to lose the fight against the F-86 and the forces of freedom!

In 1990 however, Jim procured a new Mig for the museum, a Mach 2 Mig-21 "Fishbed". I had bugged Jim from the first time I flew the Mig-15, saying "Jim, the Mig-15 is real neat but now we need a Mig-21. Why don't you get me one?" Jim would laugh and make some comment related to my desire to spend the entire Museum budget on a new toy, but in 1990 he called me and said, "We bought you your Mig-21!" This was really exciting news because I had trained for years as a fighter pilot to combat the Mig-21, and now I would actually get to fly one. The airplane was as great a thrill to fly as I expected it would be, combining a high thrust to weight ratio with an impressive turn capability. This made it a very impressive fighter aircraft, but also a great airshow airplane. We flew the Mig-21 to Oshkosh for the first time in 1990 and it made a real impression there.

In 1992, we transferred all the Combat Jets airplanes to Oshkosh to take up permanent residency there. I flew the Mig-15 and the Mig-21 there on successive weekends to have them there in time for Convention. I traveled back up for the actual Convention in a NASA T-38 with the Co-Pilot on my upcoming Space Shuttle flight, Curt Brown. He and I flew in to Madison, Wisconsin, because we really didn't want too much attention called to our T-38 and ourselves since we were due to launch in "Endeavour" in about six weeks. I flew the Mig-21 there several times during that week, sharing the flying with Ed Schneider who had been one of the pilots with me at the Combat Jets Museum. I was glad to have Ed flying as well, because the Airshow announcers just couldn't keep it straight as to which one of us was flying the Mig in any particular show, and they usually assumed it was Ed. I was eager to hide my flying just a little, so it was great when they announced to the crowd that Ed was flying on the occasions when it was actually me.

Most of the flying that week was just making passes down the flightline in the showcase circuit, but one flight will forever live in my memory as a defining experience of Oshkosh. This particular flight was to be an actual airshow act for the Mig-21, which meant that I didn't have to share the sky with any other aircraft in a flyby line, but had six minutes allotted to me to show off the capabilities of the airplane! Six minutes may not sound like a lot of time for an act, but with the Mig-21, it was just right. The airplane had enough power and turn capability that it could really put on quite a display of speed and altitude and cover a lot of ground in a very short time! The flight was to be on Sunday, which was always a big day for the airshow crowd, and the weather was just perfect with only a few scattered high clouds in the sky.

We had towed the airplane across from the Warbirds line to the performer staging area to keep all the starting activity safe and away from spectators. The Mig-21 is a simple airplane to start and check out before flight, involving only engine start, flap positioning, speedbrake cycling, and flight control checks. I always felt it would be a simple matter to do a "Scramble" in the airplane in 2 minutes or less, including strap-in. I started the engine about 10 minutes prior to my show time and taxied down to the approach end of runway 36 to wait for my turn. I was carrying full internal fuel in the airplane, which amounted to 2800 liters at engine start, and no external stores at all.

When the airplane ahead of me landed, tower cleared me onto the runway and subsequently cleared me for takeoff. I lined up on the runway and pulled the brakes on firmly to run up the engine. The Mig-21 uses air actuated brakes for ground steering as well as stopping, and a hand lever on the side of the control stick is used to apply brakes. This system is used by the British in many of their aircraft, but was a bit foreign to me when I first started flying Migs. I powered the engine up to 100% RPM and the airplane strained to go. After checking all the instruments, I released the brake handle and shoved the throttle all the way forward to full afterburner. The acceleration was brisk after brake release, but when the afterburner lit after about 2 seconds delay, the acceleration really pressed you back in the seat! I had been flying the NASA T-38s for 14 years at that point, and the T-38 is a peppy airplane, but it's a bit of a toy compared to the Mig-21. I always loved the thrill of the acceleration in the Mig! In no time, I had 130 knots indicated airspeed (KIAS), and started moving the stick aft to rotate. The airplane fairly leaps off the ground at about 165 KIAS and I immediately flipped the gear handle up while simultaneously leveling off at about 10-20 feet altitude. I waited for the gear to indicate up and then raised the flaps. The airplane didn't have enough hydraulic power to raise gear and flaps simultaneously, and you needed to remember to let the gear come all the way up before raising flaps or you would treat yourself to a Master Alarm light due to low hydraulic pressure right after liftoff. By the time the flaps were moving up, I was already the full length of the runway and just approaching 300 KIAS. Time to Zoom!

I pulled the stick into my lap and rotated the nose to about 45-55 degrees nose up. The Mig would hold airspeed at this climb rate and made an impressive zoom to altitude right after takeoff. I could choose to keep the climb going and virtually disappear from sight, but that doesn't make for much of a show if the crowd can't see the airplane. I always let the airplane zoom through about 7000-9000 feet and then rolled into a steep bank and pulled hard to bend the flight path back down to the airfield. In full afterburner, the speed would come up rapidly and by the time I was back down to field level and flying down the runway, I would be over 550 KIAS! I held this high-speed pass to the other end of the field and again went into the vertical to show another zoom climb. This time I needed to come out of afterburner to keep from going too high, and really needed to pull hard to get turned back around to the runway. Halfway back down towards the ground, I lit the afterburner again to get another over—500 KIAS pass.

This time I leveled at about 100 feet over the runway and approaching the crowd, pulled up very briefly to get just a little upward velocity and immediately rolled to 90 degrees of bank angle with my canopy facing the crowd in a knife-edge pass. The Mig-21 has an unmistakable planform with its delta wing, and a knife-edge pass was a great way to show off the airplane. I held this attitude to the end of the flight line, and then rolled 180 degrees to face away from the crowd. Now it was time for a hard turn, and I put 6 to 7 g's on the airplane to turn away 90 degrees from the runway, held direction for just a moment, and reversed to a bank angle that would take me back to the runway. This was also a 6 to 7 g turn for 270 degrees of turn to point back down the runway. This 90-270 degree turn was flown at a low altitude, around 300 feet above the ground, and showed the turn capability of the airplane at a higher speed of around 450 KIAS. Snapping the airplane right in to another knife-edge pass, I sailed down the flight line again and repeated the 90-270 degree turn. Approaching the center of the flight line, I pulled up and angled to downwind to set up for another pass down the runway, pulling the power off to slow down. I wanted to arrive back at show center with no more than 300 KIAS and it took a lot of power reduction to get the speed down to this level.

The next maneuver was always one of my favorite in the Mig-21, being the 360-degree horizontal turn to really show off the tight turn ability of the airplane. I banked in to the turn at 80 to 90 degrees angle of bank, pulled on the g's and went right to full afterburner thrust! The F-16 demonstrates a 9-g horizontal turn at airshows and really puts on an impressive show of turn performance at high speed (and 9 g's!). I was doing something much slower, but equally impressive because at the slower speed (280 to 300 KIAS), I was making a much tighter circle and using much less g force on the airplane. The Mig would "complain" constantly in this turn since the angle of attack was quite high, and I was using the angle of attack and g's to keep the speed from building up. You had to be on the rudders constantly in this maneuver to keep the airplane nose from slicing towards the ground or towards the sky, and I was always amazed at how tight the turn was in this maneuver. Coming out of this 360-degree turn aligned with the runway again, I left the airplane in full afterburner and rotated skyward to climb at about a 45-degree angle and turned to downwind.

On downwind, I pulled power back again and extended the speedbrakes to come back down the runway, this time quite slow at about 220 KIAS. This had the power way back on the pass down the runway, and as soon as I was abeam the crowd, I shoved the throttle to full afterburner, pulled the nose sharply up, and turned the tailpipe of the airplane towards the crowd to "Boom" them with the "hard light" of the afterburner. This was always a thrill for the show since the airplane had been so quiet just prior to lighting the burner! This turn was continued to a downwind position where I "dirtied up" the airplane with gear and flaps down for landing. One more pass down the flightline in the landing configuration was used to wag the wings in a "goodbye" to the crowd, prior to turning downwind for the full-stop landing.

Landing in the Mig-21 was always a bit of a thrill as well, because the recommended speed for landing was 175 KIAS with full flaps! The base turn was flown at 225 KIAS at full flaps, so everything about this Mig said

"Speed!". One of the real vital things about flying the Mig-21 on landing approach was never to take the engine all the way to idle, even flight idle being too low on the power. The reason was that the spool-up time of the engine was so slow if you ever went all the way to idle, that you essentially could forget about the engine if you really needed it. Fortunately, the airplane had a built-in warning sound for you, if you learned to listen for it. At a certain point in the throttle back, an engine bleed or bypass somewhere back there in the engine compartment would "whoosh" as it opened. This marked a throttle setting that you didn't want to be at, and all you needed to do was advance the power just a little forward to get to an RPM just a little above the "whoosh", and you would be just fine. Mig-21 models that have the bleed-air blown flaps (called SPS flaps) are even more "cranky" about having the power pulled back. In these models, reductions in power reduce the bleed-air flow over the flaps, and this can dramatically reduce the wing's lift. You can really scare yourself quite well by pulling power back abruptly! This particular Mig-21 was a Mig-21PF and didn't have the blown flaps, so I didn't scare myself that way.

Into the flare, I eased the power back very slowly and slowed the airplane down all the way to about 160 KIAS for touchdown! Immediately on touchdown, you needed to get the throttle all the way back to ground idle, which meant you needed to raise a little guard on the throttle to let you move the throttle all the way back. This was while simultaneously lowering the nosewheel to the ground and, once it was down, starting on the handbrake lever to get the brakes on. I generally didn't use the drag chute because it took a special table and about 2 hours to repack the chute, so I usually stopped with just brakes if I had 6000 feet or more runway. This took a little energy management, since the runway was really scooting by at 160 KIAS! I would look down the length of the runway, and meter the amount of braking I needed to stop by the end, not wanting to overdo the brakes, but also not wanting to run into the dirt off the end of the runway, and thereby look real bad! (The prime rule of a fighter pilot is reputed to be "Better dead than look bad!")

Turning off at the end of the runway, I think I knew that this was the last time I would fly this Mig-21. I remember it as quite a bittersweet moment. I was really hot; in fact, I was nearly soaked. The Mig was quite hot in the summer at low altitude, and I had a little over 8 g's showing on the g-meter as I taxied in, so I was quite sweaty! I had burned up nearly two-thirds of my fuel in the 6-minute routine. I turned off the runway with 1000 liters remaining of the 2800 liters I had started with! I felt great because this had been a really fun show routine. I felt sad because I knew it was the end for the Combat Jets Flying Museum, and the end of so many wonderful memories of people, and planes, and airshows.

As I taxied to a stop in the parking area and shut down the airplane, who should drive up but Paul Poberezny himself, in his distinctive little "Red One" Volkswagen. Sitting in the car with him was a man I had never met before, but recognized immediately; retired Air Force General Ben Davis. Paul had brought him out to meet me. As I climbed down from the Mig and walked over to the car to meet him, I felt so very unpresentable! My hair was wet and matted down from the helmet, and my flight suit was damp with perspiration from a really fun flight in the heat and the g's; and now I was to meet General Davis! He was, of course, one of the renowned "Tuskegee Airmen" of WWII! General Davis had a brilliant career in the U.S. Air Force and served as Squadron Commander of the 99th Pursuit Squadron, and Commander of the 332nd Fighter Group in WWII. He commanded the 51st Fighter Interceptor Wing in Korea (and we could go on and on...) and eventually retired as a Lieutenant General in 1970. I have to admit I felt very small meeting this great man.

I have flown many more aircraft since Oshkosh 1992, even some more Mig-21s. I have not had a flight that stands out in my memory the way that this one has. I probably would have remembered it just for the flying experience, but meeting General Davis right at the end of it made it into a flight that I will remember forever!

*Say Oshkosh to pilots and watch them get fuzzy and warm all over
while breaking into a large grin. Oshkosh, you see,
is the pilot's Mecca.—*
◆ **Nashua, N.H., Sunday Telegraph Sept. 22, 1996** ◆

▼

Chris Miller

The Rest of the Story

If you were in the crowd at Oshkosh on August 2, 1997, you probably
remember NASA's SR-71B as it made a set of spectacular flybys. On the
first pass, the Blackbird flew over the crowd in a refueling formation with
its KC-135 tanker and an F-18 chase plane. The sleek black jet then
remained in the VFR pattern—a reeeeally big VFR pattern—"working
the crowd" in an exotic aerial display until departing to the southeast,
seeking the tanker for more fuel. The final act of this dazzling display
would have punctuated the whole event. The plan called for NASA test
pilot Rogers Smith and his backseater, Robert Meyer to rock Oshkosh
with the Blackbird's twin sonic booms as they blasted up to 80,000 feet
for the dash back to California. That was the plan anyway.

This Oshkosh Memory begins in southern California, on a bright, clear
Mojave Desert Saturday morning. At the NASA Dryden Flight Research
Center, the office buildings and hangars are nearly silent as Rogers Smith
and his RSO, Robert Meyer, prepare to don their gold-colored full-
pressure "space" suits in the life-support shop. (In NASA language,
"RSO" means Research Systems Operator; the backseater's title has been
changed from the Air Force "Reconnaissance Systems Officer", reflecting
the Blackbird's change in mission.) As the sun rises over Rogers Dry Lake,

the still-futuristic shape of NASA 831, formerly known by the Air Force as SR-71B 61-7956 is towed from its hangar into the bright morning light. The 30+ year-old Blackbird, representing the best of Lockheed Skunk Works' aeronautical magic, is the most exotic machine on the ramp, even by today's standards.

Almost a mile down the flightline at Edwards Air Force Base, another crew and aircraft are preparing for the day's work. Major Howard Judd of the 452d Flight Test Squadron and his crew are taxiing to the runway in an even older aircraft, an Air Force KC-135E air-refueling tanker, bound for a pre-planned rendezvous with the SR-71 over Lake Michigan. Maj Judd's crew; copilot Capt Rick Long, navigator Capt Theo Theodor, flight engineer SMSgt Ken Marshall, and boom operator SSgt Dave Francey, are joined by several others for this mission. A team of NASA SR-71 experts is going along, just in case their services would be required: Bill McCarty is an SR-71 crew chief, Jim Phelps is Dryden's Director of Safety, Tim Moes and Stephan Corda are SR-71 research experiment engineers. The tanker's crew chiefs, SSgt Chris Parrish and SrA Kevin Green, with avionics technicians John Anderson and Larry Avery, are here as well to care for their aircraft during the planned overnight stay in Milwaukee. A NASA photographer, Mr Jim Ross, and an Air Force test engineer/photographer, Capt Chris Miller (that's me, telling this story) are here to document this joint NASA/USAF flyby at Oshkosh on film and video.

Today's mission calls for Judd and his crew to depart at dawn. Smith and Meyer will take off 2 hours later in NASA 831 and immediately refuel from a second tanker over the Sierra Nevada mountains north of Edwards AFB. This is the first of three planned refuelings. After a 60 minute, 1,500 mile, high-altitude, high-speed dash to Oshkosh, the SR-71, the tanker, and a NASA F-18 flown by Jim Smolka will rendezvous over Lake Michigan. Smolka, another NASA test pilot, has flown the F-18, NASA 850, to Oshkosh earlier in the week for static display. Before the formation makes its appearance over Oshkosh, Smith and Meyer will offload a scant 5,000 lbs of JP-7 from the tanker, just enough for the upcoming aerial display. The first flyby will capture the essence of SR-71 operations at Dryden: NASA's Blackbirds rarely fly research missions without the companionship of F-18 chase, or without refuelings from the Air Force tanker. While Smith and Meyer dazzle the crowd with Blackbird magic, the tanker and F-18 chase will return to the Lake Michigan rendezvous point for the third and final refueling. This will be a large offload from the tanker—about 75,000 lbs of fuel—enough to get NASA 831 safely back to Edwards. Fully fueled, Smith and Meyer are to then perform their day's final piece of showmanship for the faithful at Oshkosh as they depart for the short trip back to California. Their climb profile has been carefully crafted to hit Oshkosh with the Blackbird's signature, twin sonic booms.

During the planning for this mission, every contingency had been considered. Alternate airfields were identified. Maintenance personnel were in-place. Changes of clothes for both pilot and RSO were carefully sealed in heat-resistant packages and packed away in one of the SR-71's equipment bays. A change of clothes? "We've learned our lessons on emergency diverts in the past," says Rick Borsch, Dryden's life support chief. "Now we include regular Nomex flight suits, boots, underwear, socks, a shaving kit...for the crews." Imagine the alternative: you've diverted to an airfield hundreds of miles from home clad in your space suit, and you have no change of clothes!

By the time the tanker is over eastern Colorado, Smith and Meyer are suited up, strapped in, and have started their Blackbird's massive Pratt & Whitney J-58 engines. Their takeoff and first refueling are smooth and uneventful. The Edwards tanker is on time for the rendezvous over Lake Michigan. As Smith and Meyer turn eastward, climb to 80,000 ft and accelerate past Mach 3.0, things are looking good.

And so the flight progresses. Mission timing is spot-on. Maj Judd rolls out in the Edwards tanker right in front of Smith and Meyer in NASA 831 for a textbook rendezvous. Smolka joins the formation in his F-18. Boom operator SSgt Dave Francey plugs the tanker's boom into the receptacle on the Blackbird's back. But the green "contact" light *doesn't* come on. Francey disconnects, and puts boom to receptacle a second time. Rewarded this time with the green light, Francey calls for all four pumps to be activated. Nearly 5,000 lbs of JP-7 is quickly pumped down to NASA 831. After only one trip around the refueling track, the Oshkosh Air Boss clears our formation into the show. The EAA crowd is just as excited to see our three-ship as we are to be there. Smith and Meyer fly a series of low passes. Most folks on the ground have never before witnessed the Blackbird's unique combination of grace and raw power. Climbing away from Oshkosh after the last pass, this fascinating black machine is trailing twin shafts of afterburner flame studded with shock diamonds. The image is burned into thousands of Oshkosh memories.

The second rendezvous over Lake Michigan is as slick as the first. This time, all of the tanker's remaining JP-7, nearly 75,000 lbs, is transferred to the Blackbird for the trip home to Edwards. Some would say this mission is going a little too smoothly.

Sure enough, the three occupants of the tanker's boom pod began to realize something was not right with the SR-71.

The tanker is westbound over the west shoreline of Lake Michigan, between Oshkosh and Milwaukee with NASA 831 on the boom, receiving the last few thousand pounds of JP-7. Three of us lay prone in the tanker's boom pod. SSgt Dave Francey has been running the refueling operation while Jim Ross and I have been recording video and taking still photos with seven separate cameras.

With the refueling complete, Smith slowly backs his aircraft away from the tanker. At this point Jim Ross and I see white vapor coming from the SR-71's left, or #1, engine. We both turn to SSgt Francey to ask "do you see *that*?!" As Smith backs farther away we see that his #1 engine is indeed venting something. The thick white plume is now miles long behind us. It is now obvious to the tanker crew that unless Smith and Meyer get that leak stopped, they aren't going to do a burner climb, or a supersonic dash, or anything else for much longer.

SSgt Francey quickly radios what we see to the crew of the SR-71. Rogers Smith "Rogers" him, saying it's normal for the airplane to leak a *little* fuel after refueling.

But this is no *little* leak.

Jim Smolka pulls alongside NASA 831 to examine the leak. He reports a significant amount of fuel pouring from the panels beneath Smith's #1 engine. "Whatever you do, do *not* light the left afterburner," he says to Smith over the radio, fearing a massive fire or explosion. The pucker factor is now up. No more flybys. No burner climb. No going home to California today.

Smith and Meyer work through their checklists and begin adjusting gross weight, an act less delicately known as dumping fuel. Smolka works the radios to coordinate an emergency landing for his stricken wingman at Milwaukee International Airport.

Before long, everyone on the tanker knows about the leak. The crew listens intently to the radios. The SR-71 is executing an emergency divert to Milwaukee. With that much fuel spewing from the back of the engine, the runway will surely be closed. We have the NASA maintenance guys on board. Uh-oh, we *gotta* get there and land first!

Picture this: You're a frequent traveler. To you, airplanes are simply a means to get you from Point A to Point B. Nothing more. You're at Milwaukee General Mitchell International Airport waiting to board the next Northwest Airlines flight bound to Somewhere-Not-Here. You're bored. You're looking out the window. You see a big white and gray Air Force airplane land, brake really hard, and quickly turn off at the next taxiway. You're no airplane expert, but you *know* something is up. The jet taxis a short distance and then turns 180 degrees back to the runway. (Hey, we *had* to watch *this*). Now, you notice green crash wagons swarming to the runway. Then—oooh boy, you're never going to forget this day, are you?—you see a bizarre-looking black airplane trailing a plume of white vapor screaming for the runway, and a bright white and blue fighter jet flying formation, glued to that black jet's right wing. The black jet lands, but the white one doesn't. You notice the black jet still spewing white vapor at an alarming rate. Then a bright red parachute pops out, slowing the jet to a halt. You wish you had your camera.

It is a few minutes before Major Judd parks the tanker and we jog over to where Smith and Meyer are surrounded by fire trucks. They've stripped off their hot space suits and are walking around their jet, stylishly clad in long underwear. They don't appear to be overly relieved at surviving this emergency and being safe-and-sound on terra firma.

A few minutes pass, however, and something happens to make both Rogers Smith and Bob Meyer smile. No, its not because they've discovered the cause of the fuel leak, but rather because Bill McCarty, the SR-71's crew chief, has just opened an equipment bay on their jet. He is approaching them carrying two mylar-wrapped packages. These bags, of course, are part of the contingency plan, a commodity currently very valuable to Smith and Meyer: their clothes!

It doesn't take long for the NASA maintenance crew to figure out what happened. In the SR-71's J-58 engine, JP-7 fuel pressurized to 1800 psi is used in lieu of traditional hydraulic fluid to actuate the afterburner nozzle. Apparently, a piston in a hydraulic pump had seized, becoming a strong source of vibration. The vibration was so severe that it shook nearby stainless steel tubing to the point of failure. A thumb-sized section of tubing broke clean away from an upstream fuel pump, thereby spewing pressurized fuel into the nacelle below the engine.

It would be nearly two weeks before NASA 831 returned to Edwards. A NASA maintenance team would be mobilized and airlifted to Milwaukee. They would bring a replacement engine and the specialized tools required to change it. They would also bring the specialized ground equipment to service the jet and start the engines. To transport all the people and hardware, an Air Force C-141 Starlifter would be required.

The largest sport aviation event in the world, it is an awesome show that encompasses an unimaginable range of flying machines from humble Pipers and lovingly crafted homebuilts to the world's most exotic military fighters and bombers. Oshkosh is the Mecca simultaneously for devotees of experimental aircraft, followers of classic private planes and the warbird lovers.

◆ **Norman Meyersohn, Popular Mechanics, Nov. 1998** ◆

▼

Julie Clark

Harrier on My Wing

In the 22 years of attending Oshkosh one of my most memorable events was flying my T-34 wing to wing with Joe Anderson in his Harrier Jet. It happened in 1987 when EAA was doing a salute to the Marines. Joe thought what I did for the airshow was really neat and suggested we do some flybys with me on his wing. At that time I had never seen anything like that and thought he would never get the okay. Joe said it was going to take many phone calls to the Pentagon but he was going to set it up for Oshkosh. Keep in mind that this was all happening right at the beginning of that year's Convention.

Joe got on the phone and started pulling rabbits out of hats. The next thing I knew I was getting ready to fly wing to wing with a Harrier. I told him that I couldn't believe he pulled it off because normally the military would never let their jets intermingle with civilian airplanes. Of course now you see military and civilian flying together at just about any airshow but back then it simply was not done.

Because it took awhile for the Harrier to make the turns in the race-track patterns we were only able to make three passes. Making passes with that jet right off my wing was exhilarating. The noise from the jet was so loud I couldn't even hear my own engine running. It was an honor because it was the year of saluting the Marines and a Marine did what it took to fly with me on his wing.

Flying formation with a Harrier might have been my most memorable experience at Oshkosh but I also have a most hair-raising experience. It has to do with falling out of the Acey Deucy Bar. Being an airshow performer I should consider myself lucky that my most hair-raising experience happened while I was on the ground. I guess you could call it my most embarrassing moment as well because the only thing worse than falling out of a bar, is falling into a bar.

I couldn't complete my list of memories from Oshkosh without mentioning my most memorable person, Steve Wittman. He used to host the performers' party at his home, instead of having it where we do now, at Kermit Weeks' Hanger. He and his wife would do all the cooking and prepare this unbelievable spread. It was held outside on the lawn at his home, which is still on the grounds there at Oshkosh. I was always taken by his friendliness. His engineering mind was something that fascinated me too. He would take the time to show me the different rooms in his home where he kept airplane parts and models he had built. I was intrigued by the way his mind worked; he had a Howard Hughes type of mind. I think of Steve Wittman every year that I go to Oshkosh.

Only from Oshkosh can someone have so many different types of memories. I've had thrilling and embarrassing experiences and I've met people whom I'll never forget. Where else but at Oshkosh!

▼

John E. Jenista

Bonanza Flyby

In 1971 or 1972 I was working for Beech Aircraft at the time and had my wife and five children with me at Oshkosh. We were camping in the North area, a little South of where the warbird headquarters building is now. It was a fine calm evening, just at sunset. Everyone had a good day and we were relaxing near our tents. The fly-in was much smaller in those days, so the campground was a compact arrangement of friendly people. One of the campers, (obviously with musical talent) had brought his bagpipes. He began to play, while marching around the grounds. Even today, twenty-seven years later, I get a thrill when recalling the beauty of that moment—the wonderful colors of the fading sunset, the serene calm of the campground and the excitement of being among so many interesting airplanes and people, all punctuated by the haunting melody of the pipes. My children are much older, now, but if you ask them about our Oshkosh trip they will say "Do you reminder the evening when the man played the bagpipes? It was so beautiful!"

In that year, Beechcraft was celebrating the twenty-fifth anniversary of the Bonanza. They had built a special Bonanza for the occasion with a custom paint job and just about every option that could be installed on the airplane. It was shown at all of the aviation events of the year, and I had the pleasant task of exhibiting it at Oshkosh. This was during the time that no commercial aircraft manufacturers (with the single exception of Maule which began life as a homebuilt anyway) had any exhibits at the Oshkosh Fly-in. Incidentally, I was able to persuade Beech to exhibit at Oshkosh only after I brought them an aerial photo of the previous fly-in, and they actually counted the thousands of commercial aircraft parked on the field.

The flyby pattern was a major feature of those times, where everyone could fly his airplane to show it off or to give rides. I took to the air on the first day, anxious to show off this elegant Bonanza. Dick VanGrunsven was there with his then-new RV-3. He and I got to racing, and Dick proved that his RV-3 is just a little faster than a lavishly equipped Bonanza. When I landed after the flight, I expected favorable comments, but no one liked what I had done. Their comments were generally that our high speed was hazard to the other planes in the flyby pattern. Now, the Navy had taught me a lot about how to fly an airplane slowly, so the next day, I flew slow! I put the flaps down fifteen degrees and flew around at sixty knots the entire time. The comments that time were enthusiastic. Most people said "Wow! I had no idea that a Bonanza could fly that slow!" I learned my lesson, and flew slow for the rest of the time.

▼

Arlene Beard

My Mother's 1928 Brunner-Winkle Bird

For years I had heard of the legendary "Oshkosh" but had no concept of what it really was like.

In 1991 Bill Turner, builder of all those wonderful race plane replicas like Miss Los Angeles, Pete and the DeHavilland Comet, called me as he was arranging the "Golden Age of Air Racing" event for Oshkosh. My mother, Melba Beard, had raced her 1928 Brunner-Winkle Bird at the Cleveland Air Races in 1935 winning the Amelia Earhart Trophy Race. Those were times when very few women were so bold as to be pilots. She had always been well known to the flying community as a charter member of the 99's, OX-5 Hall of Fame and remained active in flying all her life.

When I inherited her Bird biplane in 1987 her friends and admirers all urged me to take flying lessons and take her plane to fly-ins to tell her story.

When considering Bill's invitation I opened the Bird engine cowling and looked in at some very old parts and connections. At 75 mph this was a very long and risky trip, but this was an important tribute to women in early aviation and to my mother, so I had to get there. The next option was to truck the Bird to Oshkosh so my friends at Fresno-Chandler airport all helped take off the wings, struts and flying wires, carefully marking all parts and ends. That big old biplane looked so forlorn without any wings or tail feathers.

When the plane was loaded and it arrived in Oshkosh many of us gathered at the Kermit Weeks hangar to assemble various "Golden Age" planes. My friends from EAA Chapter 1 helped immensely as it was a big job to balance and bolt those huge wings. There were at least 8 people holding up a heavy cotton-covered wing way above their heads trying to secure struts and line up bolts and without poking a hole in the fabric.

Then the really exciting part of my trip to Oshkosh began. We all taxied down those long taxiways with our race planes and the adrenaline started to flow. Here I was in Oshkosh, on display and people were starting to look at me and I was starting to like it.

I wanted to fly Mom's plane with the other race planes during the showcase flyby but I had only been a licensed pilot for one month and I was terrified. I kept looking up at the big orange blimp-like balloon and flags whipping in the wind and just knew I couldn't handle that big old biplane in a strong crosswind landing. These planes were originally built with tail skids, heading into the wind and landing gently on large giving dirt fields. Very different from the narrow one-directional hard paved runways of today.

As we pushed out the airplanes to the taxiway, I could see thousands of eyes watching. Wow was I excited, thrilled and nervous. I had dressed in the flying clothes of the era, Jodphurs, tall brown boots, scarf and of course a leather helmet and goggles. I threw my leg over the edge of the cockpit and climbed way down into my seat piled with pillows so I could see.

As we lifted off I screamed with joy and excitement (although no one could hear me over the sound of that Kinner engine). I was up there flying with all the other fabulous race planes, Mr. Mulligan, Miss Los Angeles, The Weddell Williams racer, and a Gee Bee and they were roaring past me. Every eye in the crowd was watching and listening, being magically transported back in time to the innovative and dangerous Golden Age of Air Racing.

Quickly back to reality for the approach and "landing". Would I be confident to find the grass section next to the runway marked with cones for landing? Heaven knows you can't see out of these planes, you have to put the nose down or "slip" to see details of the runway. Would I make a complete fool of myself and land on the wrong grass or overshoot and run up and over the cross taxiway at the end? As it all happens so fast, could I "hold it off" and make a perfect 3 point landing as I was so carefully taught back home by my instructor Fred Mazzei?

All of a sudden my friend in the front seat said "we're down, you can stop "landing" now. I was so shocked as I had never landed on forgiving grass before. Now I see why all the Midwesterners say they wouldn't land on paved runways with their antique planes.

Oshkosh '91 was an exciting journey for me. I won "Outstanding Open Cockpit Biplane" and shown wonderful hospitality. All the assembling and cleaning of the plane with the help of wonderful friends was all worthwhile. The best memory was when Mom and Dad's friends came by the Bird to tell me stories of the past I said, "I wish my Mother would have seen me flying the plane she loved so much" and I was told, "She knows!"

Patty Wagstaff

Taking Pictures

Over the years at Oshkosh I've participated in a number of photo flights. Many of them air to air, and some of them when EAA mounts a camera inside my cockpit and videotapes me flying aerobatics—those are the shots you see my hair flying in every direction. I've flown with excellent photographers from *Plane & Pilot, Private Pilot,* European and Australian magazines. Perhaps you've seen some of the "stack" pictures of five or six airshow pilots flying in a stack formation.

One of my favorite memories of Oshkosh is the flying I've done with *Flying Magazine's* Russ Munson. Russ is one of the world's great aviation photographers as evidenced by his body of work in *Flying Magazine,* and also his book, "Skyward, Why Flyers Fly". When Russ mentioned he'd like to "shoot me" I was, needless to say, very excited about the prospect. Our first flight took place one very early morning in August, 1998. Russ was looking for a close up shot of myself in my Extra 300S, Dale Snodgrass in Kalamazoo Air Zoo's FG1D Corsair, and Delmar Benjamin flying his Gee Bee racer replica. I supplied the camera ship, a modified Beech Baron with side opening windows and a belly port from which the photographer can shoot straight down for a really unique perspective. Harry Greene, my crew chief flew the Baron, and the late Jim Moser graciously got up at 5 am to act as our Safety Pilot. It's important to have a safety pilot on these missions, as the pilot cannot see what's happening under the airplane when we're using the belly window; and another set of eyeballs is always welcome to check for traffic.

Russ set us up in a formation with the Gee Bee in the lead, me close in on his left wing, with Dale in the slot position underneath us. As hard as it was getting up at 5 am to catch good light, we were lucky that the air was so smooth as we were flying very close together. No sneezing please. We flew downwind of the sun then had to do shallow turns to reposition for the light. The shot was featured on the "Oshkosh" issue of *Flying Magazine*, October, 1998.

The next "Oshkosh" shot we did was August, 1999. This time Russ was specifically looking for a cover shot, and insisted on another early morning shoot for good light and calm air; and though early mornings are not our favorite time of day, especially after the late night before, when Russ asks us to jump, we ask how high! This time we put Russ in the back of our T-6 Texan, opened the canopy and when we took off in formation at 6 am, we woke up more than a few campers close to the flight line. I believe we got mooned by a few of them as well!

▼

Dave Gunderson

88 in 88

I haven't missed an Oshkosh Fly-in since 1978. My most memorable trip was in 1988. At the time I owned a Cessna 140, and the 120/140 Club was planning a mass fly-in. The event was called 88 in 88. We were hoping to get 88 Cessna 120s and 140s together for the largest group of airplanes to ever arrive in one group. (The previous record was 70 Cessna 170s.)

We all met at Monticello, Iowa and over a three-day period 165 Cessna 120s and 140s gathered. It was a small town airport and we created quite a sight. People from the area came out to see what was happening and many were given free rides. The Iowa Beef Producers Association provided supper one evening and the Iowa Pork Producers the next. A good time was had by all.

On the morning of the opening day of Oshkosh we all got lined up on the runway and took off at six-second intervals. I wanted to be at the very back of the pack to be able to see this huge formation of airplanes ahead of me. But what little wind there was switched overnight so we took off in the other direction putting me number three in line. It was so hazy that at our en route altitude of 3500' MSL, the only way you could see the ground was straight down. I just kept my wings level with the airplane 600 feet in front of me and had a nice relaxing two hour trip without ever seeing the ground. It was easy being at the very front of the group but it was a nightmare for those farther back in the group because of the accordion effect. Some of the pilots flew the whole trip constantly going from full speed to stall speed and back to full speed in an effort to stay in formation. One hundred and sixty three Cessna 120s and 140s completed the trip to Oshkosh that morning. A record that stills stands!

▼

I Remember When

I can't think of a better place to be than here at Oshkosh.
I think it is the best visual image you can have of the all the history of
aviation, the tradition of aviation and the future of aviation. Some of
the new technologies that we've seen have been quite extraordinary, so
it's been wonderful to be here. It's quite a learning experience.
◆ **FAA Administrator Jane Garvey** ◆

▼

Burt Rutan

Defiant at Oshkosh

Oshkosh '79 was especially memorable for me. It was the year we introduced the twin engine homebuilt, Defiant, to the aviation fans.

The trip there was half the fun. Making the trip with me was my brother, Dick. He flew the new Long-EZ, which really was a temporary. It didn't really look like one because it was the first version of the Long-EZ. It had the rudder up on the top of the nose, what we called the "rhino rudder", and it had highly swept wings that were really VariEze wings stuck further out. So we had this lousy, temporary airplane that we were going to show at Oshkosh even though we weren't real proud of it yet.

The plan was for Dick in his Long-EZ and my group in the Defiant to make the cross-country flight together. While Dick could fly to Oshkosh non-stop we had to stop along the way for gas. We planned to quickly stop and refuel at Laramie, Wyoming. We took off together from Mojave, headed towards Oshkosh, and as we approached Laramie I sped up. I got ahead of Dick and landed at Laramie, added fuel, and took off again in time to meet him as he was flying over.

After rejoining Dick we got on the radio and called Mike Melville who was at Oshkosh already. He had flown his VariViggen out the day before. Mike had arranged a real special arrival at Oshkosh for the Defiant. To set up the arrival Mike took off in his VariViggen between a couple of the air shows and flew westward to join up with us.

Our three-ship arrival, the Defiant in formation with the VariViggen and the new temporary Long-EZ, was a very special one for me. It was the first opportunity for the Oshkosh crowd to see the Defiant so we wanted to put on a good show. I remember we did a beautiful, smooth flowing, semi-aerobatic, series of passes, in very tight formation, that culminated in a sharp pull-up and a starburst where Dick and Mike split off in different directions and the Defiant did a turn. Then we did a rejoin, a formation landing, and taxied up together in front of an enormous crowd that had assembled.

I've still got a picture in my office of what that crowd looked like. All I see is the Defiant's wingtips sticking up from the maze of people who crowded around the airplane to get their first look at this new homebuilt twin.

The Defiant still is my favorite airplane. I spent a lot of time flying it and logged more time in it than in any other airplane. For 19 years, from 1978 to 1997, the Defiant was my primary airplane. Tonya and I have flown it all over the place, to Alaska, to the Bahamas, and just everywhere else. There's definitely a soft spot in our hearts for the Defiant.

It's now in the Stanley Hiller Museum, near San Francisco. When I think back on not having it anymore, knowing it is in a museum, one of my fondest memories is that arrival at Oshkosh and the unveiling of the Defiant to the Oshkosh crowd and doing it with Mike and Dick on my wing in close formation. It was probably the most fun arrival that I've had at Oshkosh.

Sean Tucker

The Faces in the Crowd

I remember flying to Oshkosh for the first time. The closer I got the more excited I became. I'll never forget the feeling of excitement I had when I got into line about 20 miles out. I was a little nervous because of the amount of planes but also excited because finally I was there. I had never been to Oshkosh as a spectator before so to me it was really overwhelming.

Now when I fly there I have that same excitement and in fact a little bit more because I've met many people who have become a part of my extended family. I feel blessed for being given the talent to become an airshow performer and I love to share it with the people of Oshkosh. I wouldn't miss it for the world.

Some of the changes at the fly-in have been hard for people to accept but it has been necessary to change because the Convention has gotten so big. However, the soul of the Convention remains the same. We are all there for the same reasons. We are all enchanted with flight and love all sorts of flying. It is so much fun because when you look out across the airfield at Oshkosh you see row upon row of airplanes. The tender and loving care people put into building those airplanes is easy to see.

I've had many poignant experiences watching the kids of EAA grow. When I first met them they're little kids and now they're young adults with their dreams of being pilots coming true. Some of them have gone into the military and they stay in touch with me, which is really neat. In fact, one year there was a little fellow who asked for my autograph every day. I always try to have a lot of different pictures available to sign but this one day I decided to sign my old beat up flying gloves. They had holes in them and I wasn't going to put them on again so I signed them and gave them to this boy. He took those gloves home and framed them along with pictures of he and I and other mementos from my flying career. This huge picture is now proudly displayed in his bedroom. To me that is what it is all about.

The thing that makes Oshkosh different than the other shows I do is the time I get to spend with the people. Normally I get to spend 15 minutes in the sky and an hour interacting with the audience. At Oshkosh I'm able to go to the museum and the forums and this gives me the opportunity to spent more time with the people I really care about, the spectators. When I go and speak at these different museum talks people come up afterwards and say that I've touched their hearts and fired their passion for flying. I do make sure I'm accessible to the people who attend Oshkosh because they are the reasons why I get to fly. You can't turn your back on them and I never would because they inspire me. They make me a better person because of their passion and it reminds me why I do what I do. It truly puts it all back into perspective. Airshow flying is dangerous work and it takes nerves and passion and your health and so many other elements to be successful. You really need to be grounded and those folks definitely do that for me. So I think I get more out of flying Oshkosh than the spectators do because they give me so much. After all, there is only one of me and 800,000 of them.

I get to spend time with the family of performers as well. We spend four or five days together and it is like a convention within a convention for us. We talk about new ideas, design and it is a great way to touch base with everyone on how the season is going. The best of the world fly there making it a great experience.

As long as I can keep flying airplanes and Tommy invites me back I will fly at Oshkosh. Even if I weren't flying I would volunteer there every year in any capacity that EAA needs me because Oshkosh is so important. It's represents what is right about America.

George Rutan

Pop Rutan

My ability to take in all the goodies at the annual Oshkosh Convention is shrinking compared to what I was able to physically endure in earlier times.

This is not good, because as my performance capacity decreases the size and scope of the AirVenture Oshkosh keeps on demanding more and more strength. Zounds! Thank goodness, there is now a wider choice of seminar and lecture sites, at which I can sit, rest and learn.

Each pilot and aircraft owner is happy to explain the history and virtues of his particular craft. The headliners and stars are generally happy to chat on a stand-up, no appointment, flight-line visit.

I make it a point each year to try to locate and exchange greetings with a few of the old-time "regulars".

One year I asked Bob Hoover a question about an aerobatics maneuver I remembered seeing him perform in 1955 at Castle AFB.

"The reason you never saw anyone else ever do that, is for the simple reason that no other pilot has ever done it with that airplane," he replied, exuding the self-confidence and ego that are an essential part of any airshow headliner. I believe him.

This specific maneuver mentioned is one that any pilot will immediately appreciate when the aircraft type is mentioned—a supersonic F-100 fighter. It goes like this: Plant the wheels down at the end of the runway in a landing configuration, with wheels and flaps lowered. Immediately apply full power plus afterburner, lift off and perform a full aileron roll at the edge of wing stall. Control things so that the wheels get back on the concrete with enough room for full stop on the remaining runway. WOW!

Roscoe Morton is the "Dean" of the airshow announcers. One year I was up on the interview balcony with him. Below on the tarmac was a bevy of media plus a swarm of others surrounding Lynn Helms, then the Administrator of the FAA. Mr. Helms had himself just made the first legal flight, around the pattern, in a production plane using car gasoline.

"I'm surprised to hear you say that you have never met our FAA chief." said Roscoe.

Looking at the mob below on the tarmac, I replied, "No, and it doesn't look like today will be the day."

"Oh? Just stick behind me real close." And down the stairs we went, elbowing through the crowd. "Excuse me, Mr. Helms, I want you to meet Dr. George Rutan. He is the father of Dick and Burt Rutan."

As a product of ordinary working class America, I have often stood in the front ranks at Oshkosh, making my way there by tightly hanging onto the coattails of my two illustrious sons. What is the most often asked question I hear, to which the answer is, "Of Course!"—"You must really be proud of those guys." Yes, and in an occasional self-delusional moment, I've thought, "Hey, maybe I did do something right in raising them." But in reality, I know that Dick and Burt have earned their status by their own dedication and hard work.

▼

Montaine Mallet from The French Connection

So Many Memories

We have so many memories from Oshkosh that it is hard to choose. Some are probably meaningful only to us. So, let me give you a couple and you will choose what is your favorite story.

As you probably know, it is hard to get to fly at Oshkosh. There are so many good pilots that it is very selective. Daniel flew his solo for the first few years and then we got invited with the dual in 78, 79 or 80, I do not quite remember. I think it was the third or fourth time that we flew at Oshkosh and when we came back on the flight line, all the other performers were standing waiting for us, looking funny. I thought that we did something wrong or that there was something wrong with the aircraft. When we stopped the engine, every one applauded. It was such a nice thing to do. That day, we realized that we had been accepted within the Oshkosh family. We both still remember that with much emotion. We learned later on that Marion Cole was the one who got the idea. He is such a nice man.

*　　*　　*　　*

You probably know that at Oshkosh, everyone sort of met at the Acey Duecy bar on Oregon Street. It had become a tradition. However, it became so crowded that we could not even talk with each other and sometimes did not even recognize the people who were there. In addition, all of us are busier now with sponsors, conferences etc. So, it was becoming harder and harder to just spend time together. Although we still go there occasionally, a few years ago, we looked for a quieter place. Oshkosh is the place where you see all or nearly all your aviation friends at once and it is really nice to be able to catch up. The Oshkosh before Charlie Hillard got killed, we all (the old timers, the early birds, the veterans, whatever you want to call us) ended up together in a nice bar and start reminiscing to way back when Daniel first met Charlie, in Hullavington England, in 1970. Every one had wonderful old stories. It was like going back in time. It was great being relaxed and just doing "hangar talk". Everyone there that night cherishes that moment because Charlie was gone at the next Oshkosh.

*   *   *   *

I remember the first time the Concord landed at Oshkosh. It approached, all wheels down, very majestically, ready to land, touched very lightly and went around with the after burner, so elegant. Although EAA is the Experimental Aircraft Association, it was such a sight because the Concord was really an experiment. It has not been successful financially, but it is such a wonderful aircraft.

*   *   *   *

There are so many other moments that we remember: the landing of the Voyager of course, the first passenger jet with visitors from Australia, the first time one of our friends got to fly at Oshkosh, etc. The people that you have not seen for years, old students, old friends, reunite at Oshkosh and it is like we saw them yesterday. The stories flow, the good and bad times. Oshkosh is like a big reunion of friends and we would not miss it for anything.

▼

Al Bartlett

Number Five

The first convention I attended was EAA's fifth. It wasn't near as large as the conventions we have now but big enough to have better than average fun with definite advantages. You could find and talk to anyone with no problem! You didn't have to walk too far either.

So, this was EAA's fifth convention and held at Curtiss-Wright, (now Timmerman), Field at Milwaukee, Wisconsin.

Arriving at Curtiss-Wright we followed a sign to a hanger that was in darkness. People were seated and a movie was showing the fly-past of a Salvay-Stark Skyhopper and being narrated by Paul Poberezny, complete with a cigar in his hand. He smoked cigars back then! After a couple more movies I went out to the flight line. Some of the planes out there included a Travelair J-5, Aeronca C-3, some Baby Aces, Geo Meyes' beautiful "Little Foot", and Allen Rudolph's Air Camper. The Air Camper looked kinda neat with its blue fuselage and big "full airwheel" tires, which it still has today.

What's this next ship? It's got a lot of Ercouple in it but it's a twin boom pusher and the wings fold in sections to wrap right around the prop, thereby keeping anyone from walking around it! It was Laland D "Dewey" Bryan's second flying automobile. It had a Michigan car license plate on the nose. He'd taxi it around the lot and took it into Milwaukee, where the police made him return it to the field. Maybe they shared W.T. Piper's idea that a "roadable airplane is neither beast nor fowl". (Unfortunately Bryan lost his life in his third creation. Something to do with checking the wing lock pins I heard.)

Taking pictures of the planes, for EAA, was Leo Kohn. I never saw Leo ask anyone to move so he could get a clear shot. He waited till they moved on or went to another plane and returned later. (At one period, a bit later, he was EAA's only full-time hired employee.)

Another plane that arrived was a Navion, piloted by Dr. August "Gus" Raspet. He was a world-renowned aerophysicist and some of his work reminds me of what CAFE is doing today. The work he did to the wing of his Navion allowed him more range and speed than the stock ones. His moves on Boundary Layer Control from University of Mississippi were real interesting to watch. He was everybody's friend.

There was also a cut-down Cub brought in by Charles A. Wood, an FBO from Clay Center Kansas. Unfortunately, he had to leave early. He's deceased now, but I think his son is an EAA member.

The emphasis wasn't on airshows to the extent it's done today. Of course, the equipment didn't exist, like now. But there was the old spot landing, short take-off contest. I almost forgot B.D. Maule; he excelled in that stuff with his Bee Dee. Maybe the encouragement he got at this convention helped him decide to add airplanes to his line of tailwheels and fabui testers.

One more airplane arrival I should not forget! It was a modified Stits Playboy driven by Keith Hopkinson, a Canadian who deserves major credit for getting our authorities to allow homebuilts after ten years of shut down in the Dominion.

Before closing I'd like to mention another person I remember from that '57 convention. The old timers should remember Myrle Replogle. At a restaurant, with loaded plates, looking for a place to sit we were invited over to sit with Audrey Poberezny and Lois Nolinske. We envied no one at that time.

One other plane on the line (static display I think), was called a "Miller Twin". It had two Lycoming 65's attached to a J-5 or PA-12 airframe.

One gentleman I remember was Bob Burbick. In fact I noticed he still attends the conventions. Bob was with the CAA/FAA and did a good job of answering questions when on the hot seat one evening. All was well until one persistent chap asked about building a jet, which was reaching far out at that time. He never got "brushed off" through! Of course he's entitled to a reasonable answer!

A carload of fellows drove in from California, taking turns at the wheel and pressing on bravely. Ray Stits was one of them. His first convention too!

Some others I encountered were Stan Dzik, Geo Hardie and Harold Gallatin, who had a Pobjoy radial on a stand. He ran it periodically.

There was Red Morris, who like myself, was in the Royal Canadian Air Force. Later he worked for Chris Heintz, and I heard he's now in Dayton.

There are more people I can remember. Some of them are no longer around but that's a while ago and some of us are still here. From my viewpoint the EAA's 5th was most memorable. In a spirit of compromise, I'll close this off now.

P.S. Other than Miller Breweries, I don't recall any other commercials at the meet. There was no Fly Mart, no airplane salespersons, or anything. "The Show" was a 3 or 4 day event. Everybody there was, on principle, a friend! I drove away never dreaming it would be 15 years before I'd attend my next one!

Ed Beatty

A Tribute to Longevity

"Where's your airplane?" I asked, "I didn't see it on the flight line." "Oh, I left it down at Fond du Lac," replied the white-haired gentleman whom I had just addressed. "I'll be participating in the aerobatics competition next week." This was in 1986 at Oshkosh, Wisconsin, and the man was Harlod Neumann and he was 80 years young!

Sitting next to him was another giant in his day, equally as experienced in years and his name, Roger Don Rea. We shook hands and introduced ourselves to one another but I stood in awe for this kind of opportunity rarely presents itself. We had all been eating bratwurst, roasting ears and baked beans with great gusto and spirits were running high. All around us were pilots of varying degrees of skill and fame. Around three hundred pilots in all and we were enjoying the afternoon airshow from our position out in the northwest corner of Wittman Airport. It was a fraternity gathering and as I look about my thoughts a feeling kept saying, "What an honor to be a part of this."

It had all began when a group of us from Fort Wayne signed in and took our places in the food-line. My friend Bob Sluyter and I had finally filled our plates and were just sitting down when another senior citizen approached us and asked if he could sit with us. His name is well known in aviation circles, not only because of his own accomplishments, but because he is also the brother of one of the all time great racers and air show pilots, Jimmy Livingston. Livingston announced, as he sat down with us, that he was 82 year old. He went on to tell us that he still owns an airplane and had just passed the physical required to keep his pilot's license. With that he reached into his pocket and produced his license, it was singed by Orville Wright. When we had finished eating, the three of us walked outside the tent to join the rest of our friends and that was when Livingston introduced me to Harold Neuman.

Harold Neuman and Roger Don Rea are both retied airline pilots but their careers go much father back that that. They were both race pilots and airshow pilots during the early 30's. They both won their share of races but Harold own the big one. Piloting Benny Howard's Mister Mulligan he won the Thompson Trophy Race at Cleveland in 1935. A short time later he was hired by TWA on the condition that he give up racing. With a wife and daughter to support he decided it was time to start flying straight and level again and he did until 1966 when he retired. From then on it has been loop and roll for fun.

I wanted to tell you about these acquaintances because they are special. They represent achievement, integrity, honesty and the kind of intestinal fortitude (guts) that make people great. But most of all they represent longevity with a zest for life and their chosen field that is unsurpassed. You can probably find this in any field, I just happen to find it in mine. Loop and roll for fun at age 84? Hope I can do that!

▼

Earnest L. Trent, 93

Lifetime Member

My name is Earnest Trent. I was born August 8, 1906. I've owned a 1934 Aeronca C3, several Piper J3's, a Piper J5, Aeronca Chief and Champs, two Luscombes, a 125 HP Swift, and a Cessna 170 B Model. I'm a veteran of World War II and flew AT 11's and B-25's at San Angelo Air Base, Texas.

I guess you can qualify me as an "Airshow Bum". I attended every EAA show in Rockford, Illinois. Before the Rockford shows, I attended all the Labor Day Cleveland Air Races. In 1985 I was in Farnborough England, most of the airshows in London, Ontario, Reading Pennsylvania, and Dayton Ohio. Most important, I attended all the EAA shows at Oshkosh but the last two due to my wife's illness. My love for every EAA Convention has been one of my greatest pleasures of my lifetime.

▼

FOND MEMORIES
OF FAMILY AND FRIENDS

To invent an airplane is nothing.
To build one is something.
To fly is everything.
◆ **Otto Lilienthal, pioneer aircraft builder** ◆

▼

Jim Anderson

Compass Hill

My memories of Oshkosh will always be wonderful. I first attended the Airshows in the early 70's with my dad, Bob Anderson. Many times we would fly into Oshkosh and watch the airshow and then fly home. In the last 15 years I have not missed coming to Oshkosh and do not plan on missing any shows in the near future. Because of my father, the love of aviation continues to live on in our family. I am in the slow process of building a plane in my garage and one of my sons is now working on his private ticket.

My dad is now 73 years old and has accompanied me the last 4 years on my annual trip to Oshkosh. This can be considered "pay back" for all the times he took me. My father (who has owned several planes over the last 50 years) used to own a Cessna 172 and flew it for over 25 years before finally selling it.

In 1997, my father and I were walking around the grounds at Oshkosh, and I told him that I wanted to go over to this one particular area, Compass Hill, and look around. He wasn't sure what I was talking about, or why I actually wanted to go, and said that he didn't want to go there. He just wanted to know more about what he was going to see, when we got there. I tried to explain it to him, but since it was going to be a surprise, I didn't want to tell him everything.

He had no idea that I had purchased a Memorial Brick with his and my name on it, along with the call letters from his Cessna—N1129F. These bricks are located at the base of the Family Sculpture, which sits atop Compass Hill.

I told him that it was a memorial for those people who had encouraged others to start being involved in aviation. We talked about how he had given my little cousin a ride when he was about seven years old and now he flies for American Airlines. My dad commented about how he had given another one of my cousins a ride when he was little and now he flies for Sun Air. We were talking about all the people that, over the years, we had given rides to, and my dad said, "My name ought to be on Compass Hill. I've gotten a lot of people started in aviation, including you and your brother." A big lump came up into my throat and I told him, "Dad, you are there, and that's why we're going over to see Compass Hill." We took the bus from the flight line over to the Pioneer Airport and walked up Compass Hill. It was fun and interesting finding "our" brick. The brick will always be a memento of the love that my dad and I share when it comes to flying—something that he passed on to me. We never tell our parents enough that we love them, and we know that they know, but that memorial brick is my way of telling my dad that I love him and to say "thanks" for all that he has done for me.

The view from the top of the hill is wonderful and almost gives you a feeling of what it must have been like on Kill Devil Hill over 95 years ago when the Wright brothers started this wonderful experiment that we now call the "Experimental Aircraft Association". Their plane was, after all, the first "home built". Thanks to Paul Poberezny and the many people who make up the EAA family. And thanks again to my dad, for encouraging and instilling in me the love of flying.

▼

Michael John Jaeger

The Old Barn—Reflections on a Lost Friend

This "story" is an excerpt from a dedication I gave at the Memorial Service following the death of a very close friend. Bill and I, both pilots and long-term airport bums, every year spent as much time together at Oshkosh as we could get away with. The following was an attempt to capture some of my feelings following his death, using our Oshkosh wanderings as the focus of my presentation.

My life has been blessed. One of the biggest blessings is my friendship with Bill. Bill and I go back many years, almost 32 by my reckoning. Losing a friend of that long has left a hole in my life, the size of which I am just starting to comprehend. I expect it will be a long time before I truly grasp what I have lost.

Most of you probably know that Bill *kind of liked airplanes*. And some of you may know that I have a similar interest. Our shared love of aviation was one of the glues that cemented our friendship.

For the past dozen years or so, Bill and I have kept a summer ritual, no matter what turns our lives have taken. On a particular day, usually in the last week of July, at a given time, 11 in the morning, Bill and I meet at an old barn.

I'm usually there just on time, but for some reason Bill is always a little late. And, it seems, he is consistently 10 minutes late. Never fails.

Anyway, we get together at this old barn and sit on the benches out front. At first we are usually quiet, just happy to be there, and enjoying the moment. After a bit, we'll catch up on our latest events, accomplishments, loves and problems. The silence returns and we start getting into the rhythm of this special place. We start absorbing the sights, the sounds, and the ambiance.

From our seat on the bench in front of the old barn, we see nothing but airplanes from horizon to horizon. More planes fill the air above.

The old barn is near Oshkosh, and some of you might know that there is a little airshow held there every summer. For some reason, Bill and I are drawn back every year to this gathering of 10,000 airplanes and almost enough to hold our interest for 3 or 4 days.

A sign on the old barn reads "Antiques/Classics Headquarters." It is where old planes, most of which have been painstakingly restored to better than new, are exhibited for all to admire. To be a Classic, a plane must be over a certain age. Antiques are older still.

Last Sunday, when I was visiting with Bill in the hospital, we lamented that we both now qualify as Classics. And we both quietly hoped that some day we would qualify as Antiques.

The display of the Antiques and Classics is a celebration of our past and the history of aviation. Another display area focusing on the past is an area called the Warbirds. There, you can see old military planes, most from the World War II era. Like the Antiques and Classics, the Warbirds are painstakingly restored and are beautiful in their own way. The character of the Warbirds area, however, is of big, noisy, oily, powerful machines. For some reason, it is one of my favorite places.

Bill's favorite place to go was always the Ultralights. The Ultralight area has a totally different spirit to it. New ideas are being tried. A simple form of flying, accessible to everyone, is the core principle. Small, simple, quiet machines are the rule.

Here, the sense is of the present and the future, a sense built on enjoying the pleasure of the moment, and a sense of eternal optimism. I think this was Bill's favorite area because his own eternal optimism fit right in.

After sitting on the Old Barn's benches long enough to settle into the rhythm of the show, we'd start to explore the grounds. I'd usually suggest we head northward, towards the warbirds. Bill always suggested heading southward, towards the ultralights. Seems like one year we'd head off in one direction, the next year we'd start in the other direction. And it didn't really matter, as we'd get around to seeing everything before we were done.

Last Sunday, when I last saw Bill, we also agreed that, one way or another, we would meet again at the old barn this summer. As we are all here today, it is clear that the "one way" we preferred will not work. The back up "another way" will have to suffice.

This summer, on the appointed day, at the appointed hour, I'll return to our meeting place to sit down in front of the old barn. I'm sure it will seem strange at first, but probably not for long. After 10 minutes—exactly 10 minutes, I expect I'll feel the presence of my friend's return. And I'll smile, sit quietly, start absorbing the sights, the sounds, and the ambiance, and begin to recapture the feel of this special place.

A while later, after a good cry, I'll get antsy to start exploring. I'll tell myself I should head northward, towards the warbirds. But then I'll notice the thought creeping into my mind that maybe instead I should set off in a different direction.

When I do head off, I'll finally have to face the fact that, this year, my companion will have to be 32 years of memories. And I'll feel sad, and lonely, as I wander slowly southward towards the ultralights, where I can remember, and cherish, the eternal optimism of my dear friend.

Keith Wigglesworth

Breighton Airfield

Some years ago, I think it was 1982 or 1983, whilst waiting for transport to take us back to the dorms after the Sunday airshow, we got talking with some Canadians. On hearing that we were from Yorkshire in England, one of them, Mike if I remember well, told us that he flew Halifax bombers from a base in Yorkshire on raids into Europe during World War II. He said that the finest sight in the world after returning from a night raid was the sun shining on the runways at Breighton airfield. "You've probably never heard of it!" he said.

I dug into my camera bag and brought out a few air shots taken from a Piper cub, of those very same runways. Not only did I know the field, but I was flying a C150 from part of the old taxiway most weekends.

We had about 300 yards of straight bit of tarmac before the curve. So it used to get quite interesting, but now that part of the field has been developed somewhat and we have about fifty aircraft based there, including a number of vintage aircraft, operating from 1600 feet of grass strip. Some of the exotic stuff includes a Spitfire, Hurricane, two Harvards, the prototype Ryan PT22, four Bucker Jungmans, two Jungmans, two Jungmeisters, a couple of Nanchangs, Cubs, Austers, lots of Jobels, a C120, and homebuilts ranging from the Falco down to our 26 year old Evans VP 1. I try to fly the VP 1 each weekend if the weather permits.

It is a small world!

▼

Geoff Hamence

Plane Jane

Hi, my name is Geoff Hamence and I live in Adelaide, South Australia. In 1986 I went to an air show at a little airport near here and saw my first homebuilts, 2 Long-EZ's and a Midget Mustang. I was hooked, but without the money to do anything the road to building my own plane looked bleak.

It took ten years but I finally purchased my very own RV-6 empannage kit in 1996. We also went to Oshkosh that year, I was hooked in a big way. My wife Jane and son Benjamin had such a good time, we promised to come back again the next year. But fate had other things in mind; Jane was diagnosed with cancer soon after our arrival home. So we began a battle to beat it, sadly we lost on February 8, 1998.

I did get to Oshkosh in '97 and also in '98 with Ben and my mother in tow. We had Jane's name put onto the memorial wall so that all who come and read can see her name and know she loved aviation.

In 1999 I was back again alone, and I went to visit with Jane at her special place in "Oshkosh". I cried a lot and I was joined by a lady, older than I, who also had a loved one's name on the memorial wall. We shared our memories of our loved ones together and I felt even closer to that special place afterwards.

I will be back again next year as well and I'm sure more tears will be shed as I again sit and stare at a name on a wall plaque. To everyone but a few hers is just another name, but to me she was the center of my universe, after God. Her plaque has special significance to people who also have a "name" on the wall, as they too have a hole inside never to be filled.

I now have an RV-4, VH-ZGH and I call her "Plane Jane", so my wife's name and memory is always with us no matter where Ben and I go, especially at Oshkosh.

▼

Irene "Mom" Rutan

A Cold One

I never set out to break a rule. In fact, I go out of my way to follow rules. But there was this one time.

It was early August in 1975 and my son, Dick Rutan, was preparing his attempt to break the Closed Course Distance Record between Oshkosh and Menominee, Wisconsin in a newfangled airplane called the VariEze that my other son, Burt, had designed.

Before Dick even made it to Oshkosh to begin the record, he had trouble with the aircraft's power plant; a Volkswagen engine. Dick, Burt and their helper, Gary, wanted me to go into the Oshkosh Convention early the next morning and find the guy who locks down the exhibit area because that's where I would find the Monnet's, who were in the process of marketing a skinny metal airplane powered by VW engines. It was there I would be most likely to find the tools the boys would need. The Monnet's were very agreeable to loan the tools, and I still marvel at the camaraderie and cooperation with those associated with Oshkosh; everybody helps everybody.

The guys started working on the engine, but couldn't get it where they felt comfortable enough to make the record attempt. Mr. Monnet, who was keeping tabs on the boys' progress offered to loan one of his engines. It took all day to get the broken engine off and the new one installed on the VariEze, and the boys had to work all night only catching quick catnaps in the car. That new engine was the ticket, however, and the airplane was ready to go the next morning. Yes, the airplane was ready, but I wondered if Dick was. He hadn't slept much and looked so tired to me, but as usual, he was up against the clock, and this happened to be the last day he would be able to make that world record attempt. If he didn't go, he would have to sanction the time slot all over again.

Dick would be attempting to take the world record from Professor Lesher, who had built a metal airplane. When he set his record, weight was everything, and Professor Lesher had run many miles along the beach near his home to lose every bit of the weight he could before his own record attempt. He was very interested in Dick's progress.

The day was going to be a hot one. Dick had water on board, but he had been up all of the night before and hadn't eaten properly. Moms worry about that kind of stuff, but Dick wasn't concerned. Except for the Voyager flight, I can't remember him wanting a record more or being more determined.

Because it was going to be a world record, and because it was taking place during the Oshkosh Convention, there was a remarkable amount of attention on Dick and the newly designed composite airplane called the VariEze. Professor Lesher and I were at the tower waiting for radio transmissions that another successful lap had been completed.

When Dick was about halfway through one of the laps, the Oshkosh tower guy called him and said he didn't witness the pass, so Dick had to make a U turn and circle again. It added precious minutes to the flight, and robbed precious fuel. I silently scolded him for his lack of attentiveness.

Burt came to check on Dick's progress and said, "Mom, do you want to go up and see how he's doing?" In a heartbeat, I was in the back of Burt's VariViggen in the air above Oshkosh, my eyes scouting the sky for any sign of Dick. I said to Burt, "It's so quiet, how will we know when he's coming?" Burt replied, "Just watch." Sure enough, less than thirty seconds later, there he was. Burt let me talk to Dick on the radio, and I asked him how he was feeling, and inquired about the operation of the VariEze with the new engine. After that conversation, Burt and I went back to the airport to wait.

Just before Dick left the ground on this record flight, he told me that there was something he would like to have when he landed. I told him I would get him anything he wanted. He said he wanted a beer. At first I wondered how I would get a beer to him and then realized that I couldn't. It's against the rules to have any alcohol on the grounds at Oshkosh.

I remembered there was a grocery outlet not far away, so I visited. I had them put the beer in a brown bag and went to one of the concessions at the convention when I got back and asked them if I could use a little space in their freezer. I told the guy at the concession that I would be back as soon as Dick landed.

On Dick's final lap, I was ready to retrieve the beer, but wondered what I would do to disguise it so no one but Dick would know.

After he landed, Dick stood up in the VariEze. He looked so worn and tired. The blue T-shirt he had on bore a large X marking across his chest. The sun had beat so on Dick during this record, that it faded the exposed part of his T-shirt. I was so proud of him as I watched the officiators verify his record.

Professor Lesher came over to me. He had lost his world record to my son, but congratulated me. "Well," he said, "you did it fair and square." As if I had anything to do with it.

Now Dick looked over at me. I smiled and nodded, but said nothing. He displayed his empty water bottle and I knew he was going to be very thirsty. I gave him a nod to let him know I had what he wanted.

Then I saw Gary, who helped with the engine. He was drinking a cola. I walked over to him and told him, "Don't throw that can away. I want it when you're through with your drink." He was confused, but drained the can quickly and handed it to me.

I walked over to a drinking fountain and rinsed the cola can, and carefully transferred the contents of a beer into it. I went over to Dick and handed him the full, cold can.

He looked at me disappointed. "Mom," he said, "this isn't what I wanted."

"Just smell it," I whispered.

Suddenly a huge smile spread across his tired face as he refreshed himself. I think that "soda" gave him the umph he needed to get through the rest of the regulations and paperwork.

I never told anyone I broke the rules that day on August 4, 1975, but now more than two decades have passed, and I think it's time to share our secret.

The VariEze that Dick set the world record in, N7EZ, is now proudly displayed at the Oshkosh Museum. You can almost reach out and touch it from the upper level.

The next time you see N7EZ, raise a "cola" and toast her for me.

▼

John E. Jenista

Discovering Family

On opening day of AirVenture/Oshkosh '99, I was touring the exhibits when I came upon a booth featuring a metal Czechoslovakian ultralight. I asked a question of the man standing there, but he did not speak English. He motioned to a lady nearby, who was their interpreter. Although she spoke very well, she apologized for her poor English. My grandparents came from Bohemia (now the Czech Republic), so I then tried some of my extremely limited Czech on her. In the course of our conversation, she asked, "Which town in the Czech Republic did your grandparents come from?" When I replied that it was an extremely small town called Lukovec, she almost fell over. "I am from Lukovec!" she replied, gasping in disbelief. Further conversation revealed that she and my grandmother had the same maiden name, and she was in fact my second cousin! What a surprise for both of us! She said, "Of all the people in America, the first one I meet is a relative!" I guess it proves one thing though—the love of airplanes must be a genetic factor. How else could two people who never met, or even knew that each other existed, have such similar interests that they would find each other at this huge international fly-in?

The life EAA breathes into the airport keeps the aviation community fresh. There's no place else that has one week of constant exposure all over the world because of aviation.
◆ **Oshkosh, Wis., flight instructor Paul Marks** ◆

▼

Lynn Butters
T-shirt

Back in the summer of 1982 my husband Bill and I were attending the Convention. While there, we saw a guy walking around in a neat VariEze T-shirt. We questioned him as to where he got it. He said he was from Australia and they silk-screened it there. I was disappointed we could not get one. Well, on departure day just as we were about to close the canopy, the fellow came running up to our plane with his shirt that we had admired. He had washed it and had folded it neatly to give it to me. I was so pleased.

After returning home to St. Louis, we discovered our St. Louis Cardinals had won the World Series. I purchased a Cardinal jersey and sent it to him as a thank you, along with a note. Months passed and one day we received a letter from him. He thanked us for the shirt, and said, "By the way, what is a Cardinal?" It never occurred to us that he didn't know about the World Series.

▼

THERE AND BACK AGAIN

Ken Cantrell

My Path to Oshkosh

I am the youngest of four children and I was born into a flying family. My father flew in WWII and afterward he belonged to the C.A.P. as well as being part of a flying club. Each summer since I was about 5 or so, all 6 of us crammed into the club airplane and flew from our home in Santa Rosa Ca., to Montana for our summer vacation (my dad's family and former home). It was not always fun flying in the hot summer over the Nevada dessert and Rocky Mountains but this was my earliest memory of flying.

My dad continued to fly and my mother became a pilot as well. When I was about 8 years old, we borrowed a trailer and drove to a small airport about 50 miles away to pick up our first "project". We brought home a real basket case. But after a couple years it became a beautiful 1946 Talylorcraft BC12D. I still remember the N-number. It was niner six two seven seven and we all loved that little bird. I have no idea where it is today. My mother became a flight instructor and in the T-craft, she taught my older brother and two sisters and me to fly. A year or two after the T-craft project, Dad purchased a set of plans for a Pitts S1-C. This became a major project for the next several years. We also purchased another Pitts project and built them both together.

Being the youngest of the family, I was frustrated because I knew how to fly but I was not old enough to fly on my own. During the summer before my 14th birthday, I often rode my bicycle about 50 miles round trip to Calistoga for dual in a Schwitzer 2-22. On my 14th birthday I soloed the 2-22 sailplane as well as a Schwitzer1-26. Two years later, I soloed a Citabria on my 16th birthday and received my private license on my 17th birthday. Flying was my first love and it was definitely part of my identity.

Backtracking a little, it was probably about 1969 when my dad and I found a partially completed Corben Baby Ace "D". We took about a year to finish it off and this was my first airplane. I test flew it in 1970 and started building time. It was a great first airplane. N68KC was docile, slow and fun. We painted her in a beautiful bright yellow and blue with scalloped leading edges. When I graduated from high school in 1971, my folks let me take off on the biggest trip of my young life. I left Sonoma County Airport on June 25th and headed east. I had only a few stops planned and the most important one was of course, Oshkosh! I was never in a rush and if I wanted to stay a day or two somewhere, I would. At the time, I had relatives in central and southern California and I started down the valley and crossed the Sierras and spent the first night at Inyokern. Among the few items I stuffed into my baggage area was a lightweight sleeping bag and I first used it under the plane on the ramp in Riverside. This is actually one of the few times I used it. Most places I would go, I'd meet people and talk about airplanes and before you know it, they would be telling me about a couch that I could use for the night. I learned a great deal that summer. I had a small accident in Blythe and I had to wait for some repair parts to be mailed to me before I could go on. I had many encounters with weather where I would make the proverbial 180-degree turn and return to the last airport I passed to wait it out. I remember one time in Arizona where I stopped for the night at a small strip just outside of a small town and walked maybe a mile to town. After spending the night in a motel (the only time I did this) I set off walking back to the airstrip. I was stopped by a sheriff as I was walking back to the airport along the dirt road. He asked where I was from and where I was going. I could tell he didn't believe me but he slowly began to understand when we arrived at the airport in his patrol car and he watched me load up and swing the wooden prop to start my engine. I was seventeen but I'm not a big guy and I'm sure I looked more like fifteen at best. I worked at a few different airports to help cover fuel costs along the way. I had no radio navigation on board so I relied on dead reckoning and pilotage to find my way. I saw countless things throughout this beautiful country that would otherwise be impossible. But the people I met were by far the most rewarding part of my journey. My trip could fill a small book by itself but I'll just say it will always remain one of the most amazing and important experiences of my life.

Oshkosh of course was one of the most memorable parts of my journey. I was held back a few days in Maryland because of bad weather but I finally arrived, making the important stop at Hales Corners to see the EAA Aviation Museum first. I remember seeing planes I had seen only in pages of *Sport Aviation* and met many, many wonderful people. My path to Oshkosh may have been different than most but I think my experience there was very much like any other sport aviation enthusiast. Oshkosh, to me is much more than a treasured experience. It is an ongoing dream or goal to look forward to. All of us in sport aviation enjoy celebrating our unique experiences whether it is airshows, building or just sharing good times together.

In 1971 at Oshkosh, I was alone but I was among thousands of friends with a common interest. In fact I remember meeting Tom Poberezny (I'm sure he doesn't remember me) and his dad, Paul. This was a fantastic experience for me, and one that I am looking forward to re-living a second time with my wife in a couple years. Oshkosh, for me is much more than the largest airshow convention. It is something that allows those of us in sport aviation to enjoy talking about as well as dreaming about future experiences.

I returned home on the 10th of September and Oshkosh left a permanent mark on me. Oshkosh touched me in a profound way in 1971. In my case, I was not able to continue my active roll in sport aviation because of my personal family obligations. But because of the impact of "Oshkosh", the seed was firmly planted and though dormant for decades would flourish once again. I am so happy to find that even though the world has changed so very much in the last 25 years, sport aviation continues to retain the values of old. The world of sport aviation and EAA was there to welcome me back when I was ready to return. I was able to pick up where I left off and experience the joy of building and the dream of flying my own creation back to Oshkosh for a homecoming of sorts 30 years later.

I believe that one of the most important factors in my decision to return to EAA is the need to pass the baton. I have two children that are 17 and 20 and they are very enthusiastic supporters as well. I was very fortunate to be exposed to sport aviation when I was young and I feel the need to expose them to the fact that you can realize your dreams if you make your own personal commitment. My dad proved this theory to me and I am passing it on to them. I have opened their eyes to the world of EAA and now the choice is their own. The seed has been planted once again and I am very grateful for the opportunity to provide the water and sunlight. My Oshkosh experience was a lasting one. One that I'm hopeful will be relived many more times with my family and eventually my children's families.

Trying to shorten my story, shortly after my trip, I was allowed to fly the Pitts and this was my main activity for about the next 5 years. I got married when I was 23 and started a family 2 years later. With all the responsibilities of family life, I couldn't afford to keep flying the way I had been previously. I cried like a baby when I sold the Pitts. Even though I wasn't flying, it never left my dreams. I always knew I would likely return to aviation but I didn't know when.

It was in January of 1998, some twenty-five years after I had given up flying that I was in my garage and I heard a still familiar sound of a high performance aircraft that I knew must have been a homebuilt. Sure enough, it turned out to be an RV-4. Looking back, this was the spark that rekindled my dormant love of flying and building. Later that afternoon I drove out to our local small airport and began a discussion with the flight school owner. While there I saw the RV-4 and went over to take a closer look. I met the owner/builder who was flying earlier that afternoon. His name is Jim Woods and his pride and joy is a 2-year-old, 0-320 powered

RV-4. A truly a magnificent aircraft. This brief encounter and subsequent friendship is what started me thinking.

Here it is almost 2 years later and just received my finish kit of my RV-6. That's right, I've been building for about 14 months and I think I have about 2 years to go. When I was younger, I always wanted to build my own airplane like my dad did but as I grew older, I questioned whether or not I had the stick-to-itiveness. But the more I thought about it, the more I realized that it was just something I needed to do. High on the list of reasons for committing myself to such a project is the concept of passing on to my two boys, something that I was so fortunate to be exposed to when I was young. Sport aviation is a magnificent activity and I feel like my decision to dive back into it for the second time is one of the most important choices I have ever made. I have a feeling that my life has more meaning now because I am now able to enjoy an activity that truly comes from the heart. This is where I have always wanted to be.

▼

Herb Ballou

My First Time

I am a 17-year-old boy from Montana. My story comes from Oshkosh '98, when my flight instructor, her husband and I flew to Oshkosh and camped under our wing. I had been planing to go to Oshkosh for three years before the '98 fly-in but this was the first time that it looked like I was going to get to go.

However about a month before the fly-in our family got a chance to go to Chicago for vacation for a very good price. Without talking to me they took the offer. It looked like another year of Oshkosh was going to get shot down, but in my planning I realized that Oshkosh wasn't that far from Chicago. I convinced my mom that I could take a bus to save on airfare and after some prodding she agreed. My dream of going to Oshkosh came true!

I knew my flight instructor was going to get me to Oshkosh but I had no real plan on how I was going to get from there to Chicago. I didn't even know if there really was a bus to take me from Oshkosh to Chicago, but my mom gave me some extra money and I figured that I could find a way to get there.

Once at Oshkosh I immediately found the big bus tower and all I had to do was ask them how to get to Chicago. The lady there was the typical Oshkosh type, she told me exactly which sign to stand in front of at what time and all the stops I was going to have to make. She wrote it down on a little piece of paper, and told me about how much it was going to cost. Everything was under control so I went on and enjoyed the rest of the fly-in and had a great time.

My flight instructor and her husband left on Saturday morning and I was going to stay one more night and leave on Sunday morning for the bus station.

The last day of Oshkosh was great and I had lots of fun looking around by myself. On Sunday morning I got up around 5:00 am and packed up my tent and bag, and headed for the bus tower. I was going to take a short cut through the Warbirds section, but a security guard stopped me and asked me where I was going. (I hadn't bought a bracelet for that day.) I said I wanted to go to the bus tower. He asked me if I knew how to get there with out going through the display area. I didn't really but another man was standing there asking for directions as well and said he was going the same place and would show me. I said, "That would be great."

As we started to walk he asked the usual questions, like "Where are you going?" When I said that I was going to Chicago he said that he lived just past Chicago. I didn't really know where he was talking about but after walking just a little further he said, "Listen, if you'll carry my bag the rest of the way I'll see if I can fit you into my plane and drop you off at Chicago." Sounded like a great deal to me!

So we took the bus to Fond du Lac airport instead and we packed into his Tri Pace, with a brand new engine in it. I told him I was a student pilot and right away when we got to the plane he told me to check the oil. That seemed like a lot of trust for some one that he had only met a couple of hours ago. He cleared out a little spot in the back for me to sit. With camping gear packed all around me, and some earplugs I had gotten for free at the Aeroshell stand in Oshkosh, we took off and headed for Chicago.

Every once in a while he would throw the map to me and point out where we were. We landed at Chicago Megs, the one I always see on the flight simulator. When we got out I tried to give him money for the gas but all he took from me was some granola bars, to pay for the flight. I got to our hotel some four hours before I would have on the bus and a whole lot cheaper. Only at Oshkosh does something like that happen for a kid.

▼

J. Rion Bourgeois

Dangerous Dan, The Dean of Danger

At the last chapter meeting, in July, I found Dan Delano checking out the RV-6B and inquired if he was going to Oshkosh this year. He stated he might be, so I offered to share gas expenses for a ride in the right seat. He agreed to consider it, and after talking with Don Wentz, who was flying back with Doug Miner, it was agreed we would go back in a flight of two RV-6s, and meet an RV-4 and RV-6 in Casper, WY to make a flight of four into Oshkosh.

This year, Oshkosh had a new Thursday through Wednesday format. So before dawn the next Monday, Dan picked me up at my home in Beaverton and we drove out to Dietz Airpark to load up N166D where it resides in a spanking new hangar with a beautiful polished Cessna 170 with a brand new interior. RV's are not only great airplanes, they keep good company.

We loaded a dome tent, two sleeping bags, two air mattresses, two clothes bags, two canteens, two cameras, a small stove, dehydrated oatmeal meals, four cassette tapes, two novels, and other miscellaneous items into the back of the airplane. Then we woke up the Dietz folks and taxied into position by 5:55 am to be ready to pick up Don and Doug on 122.75 at the agreed upon 6:00 am, i.e. dawn. When they hadn't called in by 6:30, we launched into the breaking day and headed north. We almost immediately reached them on the radio, so we circled over my house and woke up my neighbors while Don came on from Scappoose. Don's excuse for being late was Janet had finally realized he was flying over the Rocky Mountains in an airplane he had built out in the garage, for gosh sake, and was acting real nervous, so he had to be particularly considerate and reassuring before he left. I had taken care of the same problem the night before: assured the wife the life insurance was paid up, and where she could find the policy. Didn't take me half an hour, for goodness sake.

We headed up the gorge in a flight of two, and flew at 7,500 feet straight into the rising sun, which eliminated approximately 100 degrees of visibility, straight ahead, although the conditions were CAVU. Since we couldn't see each other, we spent the entire time to our first fuel stop in Lewiston, ID describing the landmarks off our right wingtips. "See that irrigation circle that looks like a bulls eye? We just passed it." "See that wet draw that runs into the Columbia? We just passed it." Don told us to use his "Duck" handle, and he and Doug, who we named "Dougman", were bragging about lox and bagels and cream cheese and gourmet coffee.

At Lewiston, we had to extend our downwind a little for the east/west runway to accommodate a Harpoon fire tanker coming in on the north/south. We got twenty gallons of gas, and finished breakfast. After breakfast, Duck/Don had to call his wife to let her know he was a-okay, and Dougman had to call his uncle who was meeting us in Missoula to see the RVs.

Cumulus was building by the time we left Lewiston, but we made Missoula very quickly over the Bitterroot Range where we visited with Doug's kinfolk.

Our next leg was a long one to Casper. By the time we left Missoula early in the PM, there was some weather east of us. We kept climbing, and the cumuli-nimbi kept building, and we kept climbing, until at 12,000 feet we had one last ridge to cross running east west into the cloud cover, which pretty much ran north-south. We were heading southeast, and it looked to me like the ridge was pretty much the end of that route, being above us and running into the cloud cover, so I piped up, "Dan, it doesn't look like we can make that ridge." "I just want to take a peek," says Dan. "Looks like just more clouds beyond it," says I. Silence from the left seat.

Approaching the ridge at 180 mph, and still below it, my eyes glued to the ridgeline, "I think we better turn back, I don't think we can make that ridge," says I. "Just want to take a peek," comes back from the left seat.

Closer and closer we come, still below the ridgeline, still no indication we'll deviate from impending doom, I look over at Dan and he's gone! Sitting at the controls is DANGEROUS DAN, DEAN OF DANGER, AND HIS HAIR IS ON FIRE! Fifty feet from the ridge top, we peek over solid clouds then do a vertical turn to our left, look up, and see Duck doing the same to his right.

There is a huge valley running south into the Rockies, which I believe to be the Wind River Range, but the clouds are still coming in from the east. They would fill the valley mouth if we go in, but we turn and run south into the valley of the shadow of death, but it turns east and it's clear beyond, and I'm looking down on lakes I fished almost twenty years ago. That was some adventure, then. Never did it occur to me way back when that someday I'd fly above those lakes at 180 mph in a homemade airplane with Dangerous Dan laughing in the face of death and chattering on 122.75 with other damn fools about mountain goats and looking for a way out of the mountains while we still have gas.

We landed in the face of a thirty-mile wind at Casper under perfectly clear skies. Then we took a stroll across the North Platte River, and had dinner at the newest restaurant in town, which may also be the best. The beer and seafood was mediocre, but the beef was excellent. We were asleep before dark.

Tuesday morning early, we are ready to launch, but Don's starter wouldn't turn the engine over. Dangerous Dan hops out and props it while Don engages the starter, and eventually it starts.

Dan lets me do most of the flying this leg, but I fail to switch tanks. He takes over just as we approach Huron, SD for gas and brunch, and the engine quits on downwind due to a dry right tank, but starts right back up after he switches to the left tank.

On the ground, Don's left brake was mushy, so he borrows wrenches and an oil can with flexible spout to fill and bleed the line. The spout won't reach low enough, so I lend a helping hand and break it off. Hitching a ride in to the local NAPA store, I get the lowdown on Huron from the cross-country mail truck driver. He thinks Huron is dying because the interstate passed it by, but I find all six counter persons busy in the NAPA store, and my driver is also complaining about Californians moving into the area and driving up real estate values, so it seems to me they are doing okay. Don and I finish fixing the brakes, wolf brunch, Dangerous Dan props Duck, and we launch for La Crosse, WI.

East of Huron, things are still flat, brown and hazy, but as the ground starts greening up, the cumulus clouds start building and getting thicker. We climb to 9,500 to get over them, and can still see the occasional town or city through the breaks. However, we lose sight of Duck and Dougman and our other two flight members, and can't see enough of the ground to describe location on 122.75. Instead we start describing clouds. "See that big spiky cloudy to the left of the three squat ones in a row? We just passed it on the right." Real intelligent stuff, but lots of other Oshkosh bound planes are broadcasting position fixes almost as silly. Everybody on 122.75 is heading to Oshkosh and high with anticipation.

We climb to 11,500 to stay above the clouds, but don't want to get any higher without supplemental oxygen. The cloud cover is also getting thicker, with large columns growing up to about 15,000 feet above an almost solid base that extends from 3,000 to 10,000, so we decide to go down below it. I find a tunnel running to the south along the eastern side of a huge column and DIVE down the tunnel to the open air below the base, dropping from clear sky blue and pure cloud white to the gray and green of rain soaked Minnesota or Wisconsin. WHAT A RUSH!

The next hour is the easiest navigation of the whole trip as our track is exactly down the section lines. Duck starts heading into La Crosse, which is a beautiful town with a beautiful airport, both on the Mississippi. Lots of new residential construction is visible from the air. Dan makes a perfect landing, but turns the wrong way off the runway, so Don beats us to the pumps.

On the ramp, we brief for the approach into Oshkosh. The published procedure is to fly single file up the tracks, with those who can maintain 90 mph at 1,800 feet, and those that can only maintain 130 mph at 2,300 feet.

At Fisk, the controllers give you instructions, and you are to only wag your wings, and stay off the radio. Overflying Ripon towards the SE gives us an opportunity to expand or constrict a circle, and ease into the traffic. We drop back into single file, overfly Ripon to the SE, circle back around to the West, then fly NE over Ripon to pick up the railroad tracks.

A polished Lockheed Electra overflies us just before Fisk. The controller instructs Dan and I to follow the Electra for a right downwind for runway 27. They tell Dan to put it on the numbers, and he does, and gets a "good job RV-6" from the controllers. WE HAVE LANDED AT AIRPLANE MECCA! The weather immediately begins to clear.

Dan had the foresight to prepare a SHOWPLANE CAMPING sign and I hold it up and waggle it at every ground person, and they wave us on.

I had heard horror stories about getting into Oshkosh and the crowds and the lousy weather, but this year it is all perfect. Tuesday night is clearing and cool, Wednesday is clear and mid—70's. Dan and I get a shower after only a twenty-minute wait. Dangerous Dan and I almost crashed the women's shower, heading for one of the doors without a line, but a lady straightened us out just in time. "You realize this is the women's trailer, DON'T YOU?" Oops. We just assumed that since the first door said "Women", the next one must be the "men's". The trailers have a door on each end, but each trailer only serves one sex. Where are those controllers when you need them? You can't expect a guy to read every sign.

The convention doesn't officially open until Thursday, so we spend Wednesday at the EAA's Eagle Hangar museum, Pioneer Airport. The museum is awesome! It has everything you would imagine except for an RV. Looking at the homebuilt section, which has Lancair, Rutan, Pitts and Wittman examples, you can sense the gap. The prototype RV-3 our chapter is rebuilding for donation will be a definite plus.

I discovered that the Duckworks landing lights Don Wentz developed has been done before: check out the landing lights on the XP-51 prototype; exactly like Don's, except the lower cutout is slightly tear shaped towards the fuselage. So it appears Don's lights will make my RV-4 more like a P-51 rather than less. Hot damn!

We had a brief rain shower Wednesday afternoon, but then it clears up for the "golden hour" which I use to advantage to check out all the showplanes and some of the warbirds before the crowds of groundlings arrive. On the way back to camp, I fall in step with a controller. They have hundreds of volunteers to fill a couple of dozen positions, and love handling the Convention, even though they work like dogs. They estimated 6,000—7,000 planes on the field when it closed Wednesday night, and expected another 2,000 to fly in Thursday. Showplane Camping was not filled up, and in fact never fills up, but itinerant camping was already filled up Wednesday afternoon before the Convention opened.

We eat a rubber chicken dinner Wednesday night at the Hangar Cafe, and are entertained at the Theater in the Woods by a comedian who tells stories around sound effects that he makes with his mouth. Hilarious.

Big straight lines of Port-a-Potties are everywhere at Oshkosh. They are also constantly being serviced. I always thought they carried them away when they were full for servicing. I'm in one doing my business and reading a book when I hear a monster truck drive up, the potty doors start slamming and the whole line starts shaking. My god, I thought, they're gonna carry me off! I had to get outta there fast, and check out the operation. I learned that they don't carry 'em off. They come around once a day with a big tank truck and a four-inch hose and suck'em out.

Thursday morning at 6 am, the sound effects comic wakes everyone up with his impression of a big Pratt & Whitney or Wright Cyclone radial engine starting up, then switches over to yodeling. He did this every morning we were there. Bizarre.

Don had located his starter vendor on Wednesday, who had agreed to replace his starter if Don would troubleshoot his solenoids and starter circuit. Thursday morning, Don takes off his cowl, and RV builders are drawn like moths to a flame. Between answering questions about this and that, mostly about the fuel injection system, we troubleshoot the starter system. When you turn the key, the solenoid pushes the Bendix gear out, but it hangs up on the starter ring. We remove the starter, and ran it. Seems to work okay, so we reinstall it, but increase the teeth engagement space with washers. The Bendix gear still hangs up on the starter ring. We bypass the master solenoid. Still no joy. So we take off the starter, find the vendor at his plane in Showplane Parking, and obtain the replacement.

All the booths are open now, so Duck and I take in the exhibits and check out all the displays. It is too far to hike back to the planes, so we take turns carrying the starter. Don begins a long quest for a hot pink hat with his aircraft type and N-number on it. He gets a free pin from his fuel injection system vendor for standing at the booth praising the system. They should have given him a hot pink hat to pin it on for taking off his cowl.

We have a great view of the airshow right by our planes. Luckily we are parked next to high wing jobs, and have the benefit of their shade. A couple named Ron and Nancy in a 180 parked next to Don. They loan us their tools for starter work, and their shade for the air show.

Packed the cell phone all the way so I wouldn't have to stand in line to phone home and the office, but couldn't get it to work Wednesday or Thursday. Friday night someone tells me you have to call Cellular One and register to activate the phone in the area.

Dangerous Dan decides to risk the field cuisine again Thursday night, but Doug, Don and I walk out to the main gate to hitch in to town. I stick out a thumb, and a sedan with two old guys immediately stops. Another sedan right behind them with two old fat broads starts honking their horn and gesturing for us to get in. We quickly hop in the back seat of the old guys' car. They are real gentlemen; pilot retirees from Kansas City. The driver is startled by a bicyclist at the corner, and jumps the curb. He apologizes for it the rest of the night, but it wasn't that close. They recommend

The Winemaker's, and we join them for a great meal and great conversation. One of them is restoring a Taylorcraft, and the other is looking for an Ercoupe to do the same. They have been coming to Oshkosh for twelve years, and always stay in the same place, which they found posted on a bulletin board their first year.

The old guys give us a ride back. The one with night blindness steers and works the pedals, and the other guy tells him when and where to turn. Now I can see why the bike startled him. It would have been simpler if the guy who could see had both steered and navigated. Less fun, though. Dropped us off right at the front gate. A couple of tent vendors are still open. Don and I buy T-shirts for the families.

At 10 PM I can finally get to the pay phone 100 yards from the tent and call home. I'm alone under a streetlight surrounded by classic airplanes and almost total silence, just a few tunes drifting over the fence from the road RV's over by Ollie's Barn. Beautiful. I punch in 25 digits at the appropriate tones, and am talking with my loved ones. Groovin'.

Friday morning, I'm up extra early to beat the line to the shower. Second day of the Convention, and I get in without a wait at the fixed base shower next to the Hangar Cafe. Less luxurious than the trailer showers, though. Feeling like an old hand that knows all the ropes.

Friday, I spoke with the pilot of the Harrier jet. One of the duties of the military pilots who fly military aircraft in airshows is to stand in front of their plane and let the general public ask them stupid questions. They are under strict orders to be polite. I decide to test him. "Have you seen that Arnold Schwarzenegger movie, 'True Lies'," I ask. He answers, obviously for the hundredth time, "Yes, sir, I did."

"So what did you think of the Harrier jet scenes; were they realistic?"

He draws a deep breath, and fires away:

"The only real jets are the ones in the long shot, attacking the bridge. The Harrier the actor flew was a mockup dangling from a crane."

"The military pilots you saw on the ground were real Air Force, but they were ground crewmen."

"If you tried to ride on the back of a Harrier like the terrorist did, you would get sucked into an engine."

"You can't fire the guns in hover. It would knock the plane over."

"If you did fire the number of rounds into a skyscraper that the actor did, it wouldn't just knock out the windows, furniture, and interior walls, it would cut the building in half."

"Anything else, sir?" He smiles courteously.

"No, thank you Captain, I believe you've covered it, thank you very much," says I, and beat a hasty retreat. He is obviously well prepared for sniper fire.

After the buzz job by the Harrier pilot, I return to camp to see what the others are up to, and find Dougman relaxing in the shade of Ron and Nancy's 180 wing reading his book. I pull up a lawn chair and pull out my sci-fi thriller and join him. The conditions are perfect: sunny skies, mid-80's, slight breeze, aircraft sound surrounds us and a good book.

When I get tired of reading, I mosey back through the fly-market for the third time, filling in any gaps. Since we are leaving the next day, the purse strings are a little looser and I succumb to the charms of a 2" diameter flat-head rivet set even bigger than the one Randall found at Boeing surplus and some neat little MS hose brackets. I also finally find a hat vendor who will sell baseball caps with your aircraft type and N number ironed on for a reasonable price. I have one each done for Dangerous Dan and me in a nifty tie-dyed blue, and almost get one for the Duck in hot pink, but when I ask for it, the vendor mentioned another guy had purchased two the same atrocious color earlier that afternoon. "Was he stocky, baby-faced, and slow-talking?" I asked, describing the Duck. "Yeah, that's him," confirmed our vendor. "Never mind, then, he's beaten me to it."

I give up my quest for the holy grail (a mid-time Lycoming less expensive than my best car) and play a quick game of Port-a-Potty etiquette (place 13 potties in a semi-circle, form two long, anxious, unisex lines, and watch the faces, or feet, at the head of the lines when the 7th potty vacates) before passing over into the warbird compound. These aircraft are staged in descending order from the flightline according to desirability. At the front are the WWII fighters, and at the back the liaisons. Just about in the middle I find a long row of Cessna Mixmasters painted up like the one in the "Danny Glover saves Gene Hackman in Vietnam" movie.

Probably the most numerous warbird is the North American trainer: the T-6—SNJ—Harvard. After years of pictures of Grand Champion Warbirds in *Sport Aviation*, I find one here in the flesh. Every piece has been removed, cleaned or replaced, painted, and then reassembled. Painted in Harvard colors, it could not have looked this good when it left the factory floor fifty years ago. Only 6 hours on the restoration, it reeks of expense and excess. Personally, I prefer the original, experimental, concept of aircraft the EAA grew up around: affordable aircraft available to every man. But I guess it wouldn't be politically correct to exclude millionaires from the club.

The next morning, Saturday, the third day of the convention, Dan gets up at the proverbial crack of dawn, and goes to get our departure briefing. We break camp quickly and load everything into the RV's. The plan is to make a quick leg to Portage, Wisconsin for breakfast, and plan the return there. We hail a linesman, and he directs us out to the taxiway on his scooter, with the Duck and Dougman following Dangerous Dan and Shagman. We get up to the intersection, and do our runup. I look over and see the Duck is out of his cockpit with the engine shutdown and doing field repairs. Seems he left the top piano hinge wires out when he put his cowl back on after replacing the starter, and noticed it when he went to higher RPM's for the runup. A KR-2, Christen Eagle, and Avid Flyer are backing up behind him, and the controller directs them around us. The Duck finishes installing his cowl, gets back in, and we take off as a flight of two RVs for Portage. We can't see any clouds because the humidity is 150 percent. Pure pea soup. We stay at 2500 feet so we can see the ground. We make Portage in short order, fill up for gas, and ask the FBO to hail a cab, which she does on the same radio she uses for Unicom. Her office is the first wood-paneled Quonset hut I've ever seen.

We ask the cabby to take us to a good breakfast, and he drops us off at a cafe on Main Street, Middle America. Lots of old brick buildings, high curbs, baseball caps, plaid shirts, down vests, and jeans. The waitress is jocular, the sausage the best of the whole trip, and the coffee the most welcome. Revived, we catch a cab back to the airport, and at the gas pumps, where we paid $1.95 per for 12.5 gallons, see the most Rube Goldbergesque homebuilt ever. The wings are salvaged from a production plane, to which the builder has attached two square wooden booms that run back to a square horizontal stab with twin rudders. The fuselage is a VERY rough fiberglass shell with a VW engine in pusher configuration. I am surprised the FAA would sign off on it, but it has and the pilot is from Texas in Wisconsin, so I guess it is airworthy, although it sure didn't look it. Two Long-EZ's are also filling up on the way to Oshkosh, which feels strange. For us, the Convention is over, and it seems out of time for others to be still heading in.

I take all of our WAC charts and anchor them with rocks across a picnic table. Dan plots three legs as our planned course for the day: Stefan Memorial, NE, Torrington, WY, and Rawlins, WY. We agree to evaluate our condition at Rawlins and decide then whether or not to go further. We had originally planned to try to make it in one day, but our late breakfast made that unlikely. Once airborne, Dan and I put a George Strait tape on, and are singing along to "The Cowboy Rides Away". I hit the push-to-talk button at the chorus to share the mood with Dougman and the Duck, and a stranger's voice comes back on 122.75, "Don't quit your day job."

It is a long leg to Stefan Memorial in east Nebraska, just outside of Norfolk, where we got fuel, then right back into flying another long leg to Torrington, Wyoming, just over the Nebraska/Wyoming border where we intersect the Oregon Trail. We had climbed to altitude over Nebraska, but when we got to Torrington, the terrain has risen so much, we don't have to descend to pattern altitude. As usual, Dan leads, and the Duck is right behind us. When Dan and I pull up at the pumps, Don is still out at the approach end of the runway, stopped. He starts rolling and taxis in.

I walked over as they climb out and start looking over the airplane. Don had failed to coordinate his mixture and throttle with the altitude and the heat, and his engine quit about ten feet above the runway. "Seemed kinda weird to see that big wooden blade standing still while we're airborne. I pushed the stick forward, but we still landed kinda hard." The only damage was a creased gear fairing and two pairs of shorts.

We saddled right back up for a short leg to Rawlins, WY. This leg over Wyoming, had scattered thunderstorms, and grass fires from lightning strikes. One big thundercell is right in our loran course. There is a gap in the middle. Dangerous Dan's hair starts smoking, and he suggests over 122.75 that we shoot the gap. The Duck refuses to follow us, and since our lorans have been sporadic in the mid-continent gap, we turn right to stay with the Duck. A few minutes later, I look over past Dan and the gap is filled with lightning streaks.

At Rawlins, we land just as the FBO is getting ready to close for the day. Rawlins is not much more than a way stop on Interstate 80 without a tree in miles. Its major industries are oilrigs and motels. I want to push on to Pinedale, where I spent some time in my youth, or Big Piney, both of which are more scenic, but the others have had enough, so we call a motel van and head in to town.

We had planed to get an early start the next morning, but the restaurant across the street doesn't open until 8 am, so we got the motel van to drive us to a truck stop for breakfast. After breakfast, we called the motel to tell them that the four pampered pilots are ready for the van again. We can see the airport across a little valley from where we are standing, which makes the thirty-minute wait for the van especially frustrating. We finally get airborne on a cool, windy, overcast, morning and fly all the way to Burley, ID where we land in warm bright sunlight. Burley is a beautiful little town on the Snake River surrounded by irrigated cropland. The Duck appeared to be right behind us, but can't find the airport and lands several minutes after us. There are two FBO's on the airport, one of which does restorations. I'm out walking around when the Duck and Dougman finally taxi in. Dan and I check out a Taylorcraft our FBO is restoring. We also look over the wreck of a huge cropduster with a big radial that is resting on a flatbed behind a hangar. It is the worst damage I have ever seen to an airplane. Two of the jugs were ripped clean off the engine, and one of the wings had been torn in two by a tree.

There isn't a cloud in the sky when we blast off from Burley for our last leg across Oregon. Dan is letting me do most of the flying at altitude. The air is so calm this leg, I can't keep my eyes open, and have to give the controls to Dan so I can nap. Guess I better put an autopilot in my RV-4 if I intend to do any long cross-countries solo. We have finally gotten the formation flying down, and don't loose sight of each other until we split up at Mount Hood, saying our good-byes on 122.75. The Cascades seem like a major obstacle for my Champ, but in Dan's RV, we cross them in what seems a nanosecond. At the crest, we reduce power for a long glide in to Aurora. At the little FBO at the south end of the runway a young couple are sprucing up the grounds and the building. A fancy German glass motor-glider lands as we are filling up. Then we jump back in and hop over to Dietz, transfer the gear to Dan's car, and all too soon, the trip is over.

When Dan drops me off at home, the wife is outside washing her car and talking to the elderly gent who is our neighbor. I tell him I have just come home from an airplane convention, and he tells me I should have been home last Saturday: "Some fools in an airplane kept circling overhead at 6:30 in the morning and woke me up." "Is that so? Wonder who it coulda been?"

Thank you Dan Delano.

▼

The Pilgrimage to Oshkosh

The Fly Baby was an award winner in EAA during the early sixties. Peter M. Bowers of Settle, Washington designed the aircraft and to date there has been over 500 built. The emphasis was on an aircraft that could be built by a person having average shop skills and using a minimum of certified aircraft materials. The wings will fold and the aircraft will fit in a standard single car garage. The construction is mainly wood covered with fabric. The one flown by Eric Whittred has a pressure cowl and enclosed canopy, which was not on the original design but allows for a longer operating season in Canada. An 85 HP Continental engine powers it. Top speed is 80 MPH and it cruises at 70.

Oshkosh! To some this word is meaningless. To the student of geography it is a town in Wisconsin. To that group who build and fly their own aircraft it is a Mecca to be visited. It is the headquarters of the Experimental Aircraft Association. From humble beginnings of a small group of enthusiasts who met in a garage it is now an organization whose membership is now in the hundreds of thousands and is international in nature. The annual convention is held at Wittman field in Oshkosh, Wisconsin the first week in August and is now probably the biggest airshow in the world. If you are building an aircraft or are planning to build it offers a lot in technical know-how. There are forums on every aspect of design and construction. You get to meet people building the same design as you are and you can exchange ideas and suggestions. There is also a daily airshow involving some of the most outstanding flying imaginable.

When I first started construction of my homebuilt airplane called a Fly Baby I never dreamed it would make the three thousand mile round trip to Oshkosh. I had visions of Sunday flights to local fly-ins of perhaps fifty to one hundred miles but nothing more.

Building the airplane took more time than I care to admit and flying off the restrictions plus repairs from a minor accident also took their toll in time. The paper work and frustrations with government agencies also added to delays and with all these problems on my mind I wasn't thinking in terms of long cross country flights as the airplane wasn't ready and I wasn't psychologically ready.

One night while a group of us were working on our club project someone suggested that we fly to Oshkosh as a group.

Glen Clarke and his wife, Kay, were nearing the restoration of a Piper J3 Cub and Vic Kucinskas was reworking a Jodel D-11 that he had bought.

I had twenty-five hours on my Fly Baby and fifty was necessary to remove the initial restrictions. I heard a rumor that new regulations had come out which only required twenty-five hours with a certified engine and as I had a certified engine I was delighted to think that I now qualified.

So we all got together and had a briefing session with maps and charts to plan our route and it seemed as if everything was going to come together. We even had room reservations at Oshkosh.

To be sure of the regulations I dropped into the local Transport Canada office and found to my disappointment that, although new regulations were being considered, they were not yet in effect. I would have to show fifty hours in my log to qualify which meant I would have to get another twenty-five hours in before I could go beyond the 20 mile limit from base.

Twenty-five hours doesn't sound like much but when you consider that you only fly one or two hours on a weekend it takes awhile. To make a long story short, I did not get my twenty-five hours in, Glen did not finish the Cub in time and Vic was sill doing modifications on the Jodel by the time the deadline rolled around. Since none of us made it we decided to aim at the following year.

For the next year I plugged away at getting the hours in whenever possible. Glen and Kay spent their time on the Cub and Vic was finding a few extra things that needed doing on the Jodel such as adding big enough fuel tanks to make it "non-stop" to Oshkosh.

About May we really got serious. We ordered ELT's (Emergency Locator Transmitters) and I put my radio in the shop to have new crystals put in it for Oshkosh Tower and Calgary Tower frequencies. The annual CCI (Condition and Conformity Inspection) had to be done with its attendant paperwork and finally the fifty hours were flown off and an application was submitted to DOT (Department of Transport) to have the restrictions lifted. There was some hassle over the gross weight but I had the paperwork to win that round. The next round went to the government, as I did not have a current radio license so my application went in to the Department of Communications as well as the forty-dollar fee of course. The third round went to DOT, as the ELT's still had not arrived.

At this point the family holiday came up and I took off for British Columbia with my wife and daughter in our trailer. I still had quite a few last minute things to fix up or adjust on the airplane. These would have to wait until the week between the time we came home and the date of departure for Oshkosh.

Robbie Burns once said, "The best laid plans of mice and men...", and he was certainly right. We arrived home two days later than I had planned and Glen had been phoning as he wanted to leave the next day.

Where were the ELT's? They hadn't arrived yet. Where were my radio crystals? They hadn't arrived yet. Vic wasn't ready and I wondered if I was going to make it.

I rushed out to the farm strip near Acme, Alberta where the aircraft was parked and started to go through my list of things to be fixed and got quite a few of them done.

The ELT problem could be solved by writing a letter to DOT and posting a placard on the instrument panel saying that the aircraft was operating without an ELT as per Navigation Order 217 which covers ELT's being in for repairs or on order etc.

In desperation I phoned the radio shop the next morning to see if I could rent a portable radio and discovered that mine was ready. So back out to the field I went to install it and by the end of the day my list of things to fix wasn't all crossed off but I estimated the aircraft was safe enough to fly.

It was agreed that 5:30 AM would be take-off time so I packed my bag and hit the sack a little earlier than usual. For some reason a couple of drunks in a pickup truck decided to have a party outside my bedroom window and by 1:30AM I was so mad I decided to call the police and complain. I no sooner lifted the receiver when they drove off. My alarm went off at three and I figured that I had had about one hour of sleep all night.

I arrived at the field at the prescribed hour while it was still dark and only the two farm dogs were there to greet me. I untied old C-GWIZ and pushed her out of the hanger and was loading my gear as the sun came up. I did my pre-flight inspection and was polishing the windscreen and canopy with Mirror Glaze when Glen and Kay arrived.

I made a few smart remarks about homebuilts being restricted to day-light flying but by this time it was getting light enough to see and by the time everything was loaded and ready to go VFR conditions (Visual Flight Rules) prevailed.

While Kay phoned in our flight plans Glen and I warmed up the engines. Finally we were all strapped in and Glen taxied out to the run-way and I followed some hundred feet behind zigzagging to see around the nose and looking out for gopher holes.

We finally arrived at the end of runway 31 and turned into the wind to do our runups. I set the brakes, pulled back on the stick to keep the tail on the ground and slowly advanced the throttle. I could hear the Cub beside me doing the same. At eighteen hundred RPM I checked the mags. Everything OK there. Carb heat on and effective full static RPM 2150 OK. I throttled back to idle speed. Controls free and effective. Harness secure. The smell of grass was strong and I could see grass and bugs on the aircraft as a result of my runup. The Cub had now taxied into position and was starting its take-off run. The tail came up, the rudder waggled to keep the nose straight, the aircraft rotated and lifted off.

I released the brakes, advanced the throttle, applied right rudder and taxied out onto the runway. I checked for traffic, no one on the approach. I applied left rudder and lined up on the runway. This was the beginning of a great adventure!

I opened the throttle smoothly as my instructor had taught me years ago. I pushed the stick forward and I felt the tail come up. Now I could see over the nose. I walked the rudder pedals to keep it lined up and the speed gathered. When I applied a little backpressure and she started to lift. I was airborne. To let the speed build up I leveled off. Then I eased back on the stick and I was climbing at 500 feet per minute. Glen had made a left turn out and was heading south. He also seemed to be climbing faster than me which is not surprising since he had a climb prop and more wing area than I had. At five hundred feet I began my turn to the left to follow the Cub.

Glen was now on course heading southeast into the rising sun. The air was smooth at this time of day and the Cub was silhouetted above me and to the left. We continued climbing to five thousand feet and then leveled off. I was now gaining on him as I was faster in straight and level flight so I throttled back in order to format a little below and to the right of him.

It was time to check the map to see where we were. Strathmore should be to our right but it was too far away to be visible. I looked up but the Cub was gone and so was the sun. I was heading south. It was not so easy to fly heading and read a map too. I turned left and picked up Glen again and opened up the throttle to catch up. It was nice to have that little extra bit of speed for occasions like this. I took another quick glance at the map. Standard should have been just to the right with a north-south road crossing the railway that was running southeast. I didn't see it but it may have been below my wing. This was the disadvantage of a low wing ship. I hoped that Glen and Kay were having better luck as their visibility downward was better and, as Kay had a larger scale map because she had more room to use it than I had, she was more likely to know where we were.

Another look at the map showed a larger lake that should have been just ahead and to the left with the town of Hussar just to the south of it, Deadhorse Lake according to the map. Where was Deadhorse Lake? I didn't see any lake. How could anyone have missed a lake that size? Maybe we were lost. What a way to start a trip, getting lost in the first twenty miles! Oh well, I would just tag along until I saw something familiar.

We droned on and on. It was getting quite hot. Even though I had the canopy slid full back it was uncomfortable. My feet felt as though they were on fire. I looked at the outside air temperature gauge and it was eighty degrees Fahrenheit at five thousand feet! What was it going to be like later that day?

Off to my right I saw a highway and a railway. The Trans-Canada highway and the CPR mainline from Calgary to Medicine Hat! I thought we must be getting close to Brooks. If so I should be able to see the huge reservoir of Lake Newell to the southeast. There was something glittering in the distance that could have been it. Now I was in more familiar territory that I had flown over before. Yes, that was definitely Lake Newell. But where was the Cub? In my efforts to navigate I had passed it. I did a large three hundred and sixty-degree turn to the right and came up behind it and into formation again.

Carefully holding this position I sneaked another look at the map. We were coming up on the Military Station at Suffield. I could see the runway down and to the left and there was the town further to the south on the highway. Medicine Hat should have been somewhere ahead and to the right but there was nothing but a slightly darker patch of haze there. I looked to the right and saw the Bow River coming in from the west. Medicine Hat should be where the river and the highway joined but I still couldn't see it.

The heat was becoming unbearable on my feet but I only had room for one pair of shoes so I was going to have to tough it out. I checked the oil temperature 215 degrees Fahrenheit and we were red lined at 220. Outside air temperature was 85 degrees. I made a mental note to discuss with Glen at Medicine Hat the possibility of filing for a higher altitude on the leg to Swift Current. My thoughts were interrupted by a noise like "Zip-Zip". Had I really heard it or was I imagining things? Out of the haze ahead I could see the outline of Medicine Hat. The airport was southwest of the town but I couldn't make it out yet. I turned on the radio and tuned to 122.2 in time to hear Glen calling Medicine Hat radio. Wind was from the south at 15 mph and the live runway was 21.

We started letting down to circuit height and passed over the airport. Glen turned left on the downwind leg and I followed swinging wider to give us more separation on the approach. We were now heading north over the city and started to turn left for the base leg. I recalled doing this approach with AL Woods years ago and that the heat from the roofs over the city made the going pretty bumpy.

I pulled on carburetor heat and reduced power as I watched Glen turn final. Now I was turning final and as I let down I started to feel the bumps from the heat waves off the roofs which threw me off course a little. I concentrated hard on the approach and noticed that the Cub was down and turning off onto the taxiway. I was over the river now and approaching the cliff beyond which was the end of the runway and I was still in rough air. I checked my airspeed and reduced power a little. I felt her settle. I eased back and began my flare. I chopped the throttle all the way and felt the wheels touch. I seemed to be in the air again. I felt the wheels touch again and this time I stayed down. I felt the wheels rolling over the cracks in the tarmac. Bang-bang. Bang-bang. Boy! Those cracks must have been four inches across!

I stopped rolling, pushed in the carb heat control and added power as I taxied for the turnoff. Now I was off the runway and taxiing in towards the ramp. I applied left rudder and stuck my head out the right side to see around the nose. Then right rudder and stuck my head out the left and so on. The Cub was in front of the pumps gassing up so I stopped clear of it and cut the switches. As I turned off the radio and unplugged my headset I was conscious of the quietness. I could hear the gyro still running in the turn and bank indicator.

I climbed out and stretched my legs. It was hot and windy. Typical of Medicine Hat. As I grasped the propeller to move the aircraft up to the pumps I noticed that the leading edge of the prop was sticky. My leading edge protective tapes were gone! That was the "Zip-Zip" that I heard.

A little gasoline drained from the quick-drain valve on the gascolater on a rag and I was able to get most of the stickiness off. After refueling we walked over to the terminal and had a coffee break in the cafeteria. About this time Kay remarked that Deadhorse Lake was a little hard to find because it had dried up and she was finally able to see the outline of it on the ground to identify it. So that solved the mystery of Deadhorse Lake. We figured that two and a half hours to Medicine Hat wasn't too bad and started to plan for the next leg to Swift Current. Kay got up to get the maps from the aircraft but couldn't get out of the door to the ramp because there was no handle on the inside of the door for security reasons. We discovered that there was enough space under the door to get one's fingers through and pull the door open so off we went to get the maps.

By the time we had plotted our courses, checked weather with flight services, filed our flight plans, started up and taxied out for take off I was surprised to see that it was now 10:45 AM. Take off was to the east this time as the wind had now changed since we landed. We did our run up, got clearance and took off on runway 09.

The climb out was over some rough terrain that looked like a gravel pit or a dump and the air over this was bumpy. By the time I had gotten through this I had lost Glen and it was a few minutes before I spotted him again. Off to the south I could see the Cyprus Hills and the town of Maple Creek, Saskatchewan. There is not vary much of interest from here on to Swift Current except some large alkali lakes which seem to come and go like Deadhorse Lake and sometimes you can only see their dry outlines on the ground.

We kept the Trans-Canada highway on our right as our track was somewhat to the north of it and eventually arrived over the town of Swift Current. I recalled that the airport was about ten miles southeast of the town so we kept going until we spotted it. It was one of the typical old World War II air force bases with the familiar triangle pattern of runways. We called Swift Current radio on 122.2 and got the wind speed and direction. We were given runway 12, which meant landing to the southeast. As the wind was from the south this meant a crosswind from the right.

The approach was down a shallow valley and I could see the Cub descending ahead of me and beginning a gentle turn to the right. This reminded me that it was time I started losing some altitude too so I eased back on the throttle and swung in line astern leaving plenty of separation as I approach a little faster. The Cub was on final approach now and I pulled on carburetor heat and reduced power some more. Glen was down now and taxiing to the end of the runway for the turnoff. I reminded myself of the crosswind and put the starboard wing down to compensate for the drift and line up with runway 12. The air was not so smooth and I had difficulty keeping lined up. Five hundred feet, two hundred, one hundred and I was over the threshold. I saw the individual pebbles in the runway. Time to flare. I was about two feet off, chopped the power and was down and rolling. The nose wanted to swing to the right because of the cross wind so a little left rudder and a touch of left brake got things straight again.

It was now 12:45. Exactly two hours from Medicine hat to Swift Current.

After taxiing in to the ramp and shutting down we noticed that the wind was quite strong. So strong, in fact, that we decided to wait for awhile until it abated somewhat.

In the meantime we refueled and went into the lounge of the local flying club and relaxed in some easy chairs provided for the purpose.

A family of four arrived in a Cessna, a man and his wife and two daughters. One of the girls seemed to be suffering from airsickness and had our sympathy. The mother also seemed to be a little harassed and in no hurry to proceed but after an hour or so the man insisted that they get moving so they reluctantly followed him out.

We checked the wind sock again and it was standing straight out. As the wind was from the south this meant a strong crosswind and Glen was not happy about this as the Cub would be at the mercy of the crosswinds.

Finally after about four hours of waiting we decided that the wind had died sufficiently to attempt our last leg of that day to Regina. We started up and taxied out using caution as the wind was still fairly brisk. Runway 12 was recommended but it still gave us a strong crosswind factor from the right. The Cub got off first and I followed a few moments later with a little fancy footwork on the rudder pedals to stay lined up on the runway. I let her build up a fair bit of speed before I rotated as I didn't want to take any chances of bouncing in a crosswind. I was finally off climbing. We spotted the Trans-Canada highway and kept it on our right. We passed Herbert, Chaplin and Mortlach and were now coming up on Moose Jaw. Here we swung to the north of the town to keep the Canadian Forces base and its restricted area well to the south of us.

We had agreed to contact each other on the quarter hour in order to conserve our radio batteries but between navigating and keeping an eye on the instruments sometimes the appointed time would slip by and before I was aware of it, it was too late. We were approaching Regina and, as my little Radair 10-channel set did not have 118.3 MHz (Regina Tower Frequency); therefore, I was going to have to let Glen talk to the tower for us both. I looked around for the Cub but could not see it anywhere. I made sure that I tuned in on the next contact time and asked Glen where he was. We were over a part of Saskatchewan that had no landmarks of note and he said that he was right over a white truck on the highway. By this time I saw what looked like a potash processing plant below me and told him that I was circling over it. He could not see any plant and I could not see any white truck, so for the time being I had to assume that I had lost him.

My lack of sleep from the night before was catching up on me so I shook my head to clear it and resolved to stay alert until I was on the ground again. I could now see the outline of Regina in the haze ahead but still no sign of the Cub. I decided that if he did not come into view soon I would attempt cal Regina on 121.9, their ground frequency, and see if they would bring me in on that.

When I estimated that I was about eight miles out I tuned 121.9 and called Regina Ground. When they answered I explained that I did not have their Tower frequency and would they please be kind enough to bring me in on 121.9. They confirmed that this was O.K. with them and I began to breathe a little easier. When I was a little closer I called then again and got wind speed and direction, and started my descent and approach to runway 12.

Keeping a sharp lookout for other traffic, I pulled on carburetor heat, throttled back, and approached at seventy mph with about 1800 RPM on the tach. The approach was straight in and I managed to make a passable landing. The controller was most helpful and guided me through the maze of taxiways to the Regina Flying Club. I felt most obliged to that man whoever he may be and thanked him for his assistance.

On one of my turns from one taxiway to another I noticed the Cub was only about a hundred yards behind me which raised my spirits even more. It was now 6:35 PM, two hours and five minutes from Swift Current. We managed to get a gas truck to refuel us and tied down for the night while Kay went to phone her sister.

While we were waiting for her to show up we noticed a replica of a World War II Italian Fiat fighter from Edmonton in the hangar. It was obviously on its way to Oshkosh but seemed to be in difficulties as all the cowlings were off and it looked like a major overhaul was in progress. There was no one around to ask so we came away none the wiser.

We returned to the Flying Club where I was introduced to Ann Hamilton, Kay's sister. We gather up our belongings and headed out to the parking lot. On the way to the Hamilton residence we picked up a couple of pizzas for dinner. It was a very hot night so we sat out in the carport to eat and noticed that most of the neighbors were sitting out too. Ann's husband, Gordon, was very interesting to talk to but my lack of sleep from the night before had finally got to me so I made my apologies and retired to bed.

The next morning which was Saturday we arose bright and early and after a shower, shave and some very welcome bacon and eggs we headed for the airport. We untied the aircraft, did our walk around inspection, stowed our gear on board and went back to the Flying Club office to file our flight plans. After saying goodbye and thanks to Ann we started up, called the Tower for a clearance, and taxied out.

I was again relying on Glen to talk to the Tower for both of us on their frequency to get a takeoff clearance. While we were running up at the end of runway 12 we had to wait for an Air Canada DC9 to backtrack, turn around, and take off. I looked over at Glen and he made signs that his radio wasn't working. I was still only able to talk to the Tower on ground frequency so I explained our problem to them and the operator told us to hold until the runway was clear.

Just then I noticed that my armrest was coming loose and I was concerned that it might drop off and jam in the rudder cables so I pulled it right off. Now I had a problem of what to do with it. The cockpit is pretty snug and I just couldn't think of a place to stow it safely. My Fly Baby has rear vision cutouts in the headrest like a Curtiss P40 so I reached over my shoulder and slipped it in the cutout.

Just then the Tower gave us permission to taxi into position and hold until the wake turbulence had subsided. I tried to communicate this to Glen by sign language but he didn't understand that he was to hold so he taxied out, lined up and took off. I expected to see a little buffeting but of course he was off long before the rotation point of our big brother and was well clear of the turbulence.

I followed shortly after and as the wind was from my right I climbed out to the south of the runway reasoning that any turbulence would drift to the north. We were obviously successful as there was nary a bump and we were on our way to Moosomin, Saskatchewan.

The weather was holding well although a fairly stiff wind was developing from the south. We followed the Trans-Canada highway in general, cutting the odd corner. We passed Qu'Appelle, Indian Head, Wolseley, Grenfell and Broadview en route. We were fairly relaxed knowing that Saskatchewan abounds with small airports and suitable terrain for forced landings should the eventuality arise.

At about 10:00 AM we arrived over Moosomin which is not exactly a high density area and started looking for the airport which, according to the map, was northeast of the town. Try as I would, I could not see anything that remotely resembled an airport so I just kept following the Cub. Soon it began to descend and then turn left. I heard Glen on the radio advising Moosomin traffic that he was downwind for runway 19. I now saw faint tracks in the grass that one might say were runways but if I hadn't seen a few aircraft parked around I still wouldn't be sure.

Judging by the windsock and the waving grass and trees I gathered that we had a pretty stiff breeze from the south. I turned base, pulled on card heat and reduced power meanwhile watching the Cub on final. I did my landing check and then turned final myself. The runway appeared to be about a foot deep in foxtails bent over in the wind, which was now coming in gusts. It was right in line with an open gate in a fence and it seemed as if I would have to fly through the gate in order to land. The gusts were stronger now and I found myself caught in turbulence coming off some trees and a barn to my right. It took all my concentration to keep the plane level and lined up but fortunately the wind was right down the runway. I was now through the gate, or over it as the case may be, and started my round out. The Cub had pulled clear of the runway to the left waiting for me to land. I closed the throttle, felt the wheels rumble and in no time I seemed to be stopped. I shut off carb heat, did a 180-degree turn and taxied in behind the Cub down a dirt road towards the shelter of some buildings and trees. I remembered to push the stick forward to keep the tail down as the stiff breeze was now behind me.

We shut down, unbuckled and climbed out. There were a few T-hangers with aircraft in them and a trailer that turned out be the office or clubhouse of the Moosomin Flying Club. We found the gas pump, which was a homemade affair, but we needed to get to a phone to close our flight plan.

Just then we heard a motor start up which Glen identified as a grain loader. I went around the corner of a building and sure enough a man was loading grain. I asked him about a phone and he directed me to a house further up in the trees. We knocked on the door but got no answer. I looked through the window in the door and saw a lager Boxer dog standing in the middle of the kitchen floor and he didn't look too friendly. We were getting concerned as our flight plan was now overdue and we had no way of closing it. We were starting to have visions of a Search and Rescue Hercules out looking for us with us paying the fuel bill when a man crutches opened the door.

We explained our situation and he allowed us to come in and use the phone. While Kay was closing the flight plan he told us that he had to cancel a hunting trip because of an accident. He had fallen from a loft in the barn the day before and, although he had managed to land on his feet, he had broken some bones in his foot. The doctor had put a plaster cast on his foot right up to his knee but during the night his foot had swollen. The cast of course would not give and the resulting pain was more than he could bear so he had removed the cast himself. A hammer and saw and the remains of the cast were lying on the kitchen floor and the poor fellow had gone back to bed.

We needed fuel so he told us how to operate the pump. I also needed oil which I found in the trailer so after attending to these matters we went back to pay him and file a flight plan for Brandon.

We felt badly at having to disturb him again but eventually we got everything accomplished. Just as we were leaving the house his wife drove up from a grocery shopping trip to town and apologized for not being around to help. We, in turn, apologized for disturbing her husband in his condition and told her about the incident with the cast of which she was unaware.

Back at the trailer we met one of the local pilots who had just arrived and was also planning a trip to Brandon. He helped us get started and showed us a hidden taxiway in the grass to the end of the runway which saved us some time.

The wind was quite strong by now but at lease it was straight down the runway so we anticipated a short takeoff run. We turned into the wind, set the brakes and did our runup and takeoff checks. The Cub moved to the end of the runway, lined up, then began to roll. I watched closely to see how soon it would become airborne as the wind was now about 25 m.p.h. The takeoff was very short and the Cub climbed steeply. I knew that I would probably take just a little longer but I should still only need about one-third of the runway. I taxied into position, lined up, and pushed throttle and stick ahead together as I wanted the tail up as soon as possible to see over the nose. The tail came up and I became very conscious of the rudder in order to hold her straight. I was now past the point where the Cub had lifted off and was so busy keeping my eyes on the runway that I felt I couldn't glance at the airspeed indicator. She must be ready to fly so I eased back on the stick and—nothing. Instinctively, I closed the throttle and then thought, "There's lots of runway left. Try again." So I opened it fully again but it soon became evident that she was just not going to fly. And then the reason became clear. The foxtails growing on the runway were high enough to strike the straight-across axle of the Fly Baby and produce just enough drag that I couldn't get flying speed. Quickly, I closed the throttle. I should have held forward stick pressure to keep the tail up so I could see over the nose but I became confused and let it down in order to get stopped as soon as possible. I was now blind forward and still had too much speed to use brakes. I felt her start to drift off the runway to the right and, rather than any sudden corrective action that could have resulted in a ground loop, I let her drift. I was now in a hay field, which had been cut and the swath lay in row parallel to the runway. As I plowed through this, grass and hay flew up in all directions. I was slowing at last and the aircraft started turning to the left back to the runway. It stopped suddenly and I heard a clunk on the port wing and thought I must have hit some obstruction on the ground. I sat there confused for a moment and then started to become aware of things. The engine was still running so I cut the switches and stopped it. I released the harness, removed my flying helmet and slowly climbed out to take stock of the damage.

I had come to rest in a shallow depression at the side of the runway, which was probably a drainage ditch, and this is what had stopped me so suddenly. The plane was at 90 degrees to runway, facing it, and apart from being covered with hay it seemed to have suffered no damage. About this time the fellow we had been talking to at the trailer drove down the runway in his pickup truck. I also became conscious of cars on a gravel road 100 feet to the west of me leaving clouds of dust behind them. A pickup truck stopped on the road and another man came over to see if he could help.

The three of us were able to get GWIZ out of the ditch and onto a dirt road leading to the highway and there I went over her very carefully. There was no discernible damage so it seemed as through the next problem was how to get into the air.

In the meantime Glen and Kay were circling in the Cub probably thinking the worst. I was afraid they would try to land but it turned out they couldn't because the pickup was still on the runway.

About this time I noticed a bulldozer parked to the east of the runway an also a three foot deep ditch that it had dug right across the runway. I really started to sweat when I realized that if I had been able to retain control and stay on the runway I would have dropped into that ditch and would have sustained considerable damage to the aircraft if not to myself.

The pilot who had helped me was asking what the problem was and I explained that the growth on the runway was making it impossible for me to get airspeed and I wasn't fussy about attempting it again under those conditions.

He suggested that I try the road and before I rejected the idea I thought I had better take a look at it. It was only 100 feet away and closer I got the better it looked. No fences to get over, no gates to go through, no power lines and no trees. Only deep ditches on each side of the road. As if reading my mind he said, "You'll have to be quick on the rudder but it should work."

I had to do something quickly as the clock was running on the flight plan. Either I was going to have to get in the air or go back and phone a cancel. I made the decision to go for it. It was either that or be stranded in Moosomin until somebody mowed the runway which could be a long time.

The man who had stopped on the road got in his truck and went south down the highway to stop traffic and the other fellow helped me move the aircraft to the road. He then parked his truck behind me across the road to block traffic while I got in and buckled up and put my helmet on.

I set the brakes and the throttle and turned the switches on. He swung the prop and she fired up right away. I did a quick runup and mag check and then forward with the throttle and stick. I was ready on the rudder pedals but the wind seemed to be right down the road so things looked good.

It seemed as through I barely got the tail up by the time she was flying. I leveled off to get maximum revs and then started my climb out. I joined up with Glen and we headed for Brandon.

I was concerned about the time this had taken and how it would affect out flight plan. I glanced at the clock on the panel. 11:40 AM! I couldn't believe my eyes. Ten minutes! That's all the time it had taken. It had seemed like an eternity on the ground.

After awhile when my heart and blood pressure had settled down and my anxiety factor had returned to normal, I turned my attention to the task of navigating to Brandon. In about 25 minutes we were passing

Miniota and about 45 minutes later we could hear Brandon's ATC (Air Traffic Controller) on the radio. So I started looking around to see if I could spot the airport, which, according to the map should be about five miles or more north of the city.

Soon I spotted what looked like an airport off my left wing. We must have drifted to the south of our track. But this was not logical because the wind was from the south so if we were going to be off track at all it should be to the north. Anyway there it was with beautiful wide runways and concrete aprons and large hangers. It had to be a major center.

I waited for Glen to begin a left turn for the approach but he kept right on going. I studied the airport below me. No sign of life! Not a movement! Then I checked the map and realized that it was the old Air Force base of Rivers, which was now converted to private use for glider flying. Brandon was another 20 miles away. I recalled that one of our chapter members had had a similar incident in Saskatchewan. He had worked the Tower at one airport and had landed at another one nearby. We certainly didn't need any more red faces today. Eventually Brandon came into sight where it should have been right over the nose.

As the wind was from the south none of the runways were free from crosswind but runway 14, which faces southeast and seemed the most favorable. The tower however informed us that repair work was being done on the south end of runway 14 and that we would have to use runway 20, which faced southwest.

Glen was more than a little concerned because the Cub was not supposed to be operated in a crosswind factor of between 20 and 30 m.p.h.

He asked the Tower if he could land short on runway 14 because we would still not come anywhere near the repair crew. The Tower was adamant, runway 20 or nothing. This meant a strong crosswind from the left, so we accepted our fate and began our approach.

I watched with interest as the Cub descended port wing low, slipping into the crosswind. It flared, touched down and everything seemed all right when suddenly it turned left and off into the grass in the center of the triangle of runways. The Tower asked if he was all right and he replied in the affirmative although I could tell by the tone of his voice that he would like to have added some comment about uncooperative controllers who didn't appreciate the dangerous position into which they had put him.

In the meantime I continued my approach, port wing low, ready for any sudden gusts (and there were a few). I touched down on the port wheel, settled onto the right and as soon as I had lost a little speed I let the tail wheel down to prevent the weathercocking that had occurred with the Cub. It was probably one of the better crosswind landings that I have made but then I was on my guard after what had happened to the Cub.

We taxied up to the gas pumps and shut down. After refueling we parked and tied the aircraft down as the wind was quite strong. I noticed that the fiberglass covering on my ground adjustable prop was separating on the leading edge at the tip so I asked the attendant if he had any adhesive that might hold it on. He looked around his shop and found some semi-dried contact cement so I tried it and it seemed to work.

The armrest that I stowed in the rear window was gone. I assumed that my sudden stop at Moosomin had thrown it forward and the "clunk" I heard was made by it bouncing off the wing.

Glen, meanwhile, was having problems with mags that refused to ground but there didn't seem to be much we could do about them.

We relaxed in the lounge and ate some apples that Ann Hamilton had given us. We were now becoming aware that in flying cross-country from small Canadian airports you could get quite hungry and apart from chocolate bars and coffee machines you couldn't get anything to eat.

We planned on having lunch in Brandon as we thought it would be a major center but we could only find seven people working at the airport and apart from that it seemed quite deserted. The passenger terminal was all locked up and we surmised that it was only open when scheduled flights came in. As the airport was a few miles from town it didn't seem worthwhile taking a ten-dollar taxi ride each way for lunch so we made a few trips to the water cooler and apart from our apples we starved.

The wind showed no signs of abating so it looked like a repeat of the previous afternoon at Swift Current as Glen was not anxious to attempt a crosswind takeoff. Finally at 4:00 PM after checking with flight services we decided to attempt the leg to Portage La Prairie. The wind had died down somewhat but we were still looking at a crosswind situation. As we were taxiing out I heard Glen on the radio bargaining with the Tower for a runway closer to the wind but no go. He then asked for permission to take off on the grass but the controller was absolutely firm, runway 09.

Fortunately, it was a wide runway so we crowded into the left-hand corner at the threshold and took off on a long diagonal across the runway to minimize the crosswind effect. Holding the aircraft down so there would be no crosswind bounces.

We got into the air at 4:30 PM and set course for Portage La Prairie 75 miles away noting that we had alternate airports at Carberry about 27 miles away and Austin about 45 miles away.

All went well and as evening approached the air became smoother and cooler. As we approached Portage we were watching closely for landmarks. There was a military base south of town but we noticed in the V.F.R supplement that there was a grass strip just north of town so we headed for that.

We had cut the corner on the Trans-Canada highway by staying to the north of it and just past Austin we joined up with it again. The highway went due east at this point and we kept it on our right as the airport was on the north edge of town.

I was making a visual sweep along the instrument panel, out along the port wing, across the horizon and then back in along the starboard wing to prevent my eyes from going into automatic focus 300 feet ahead. It was approaching twilight and I wanted to be visually alert for any other traffic. As my eyes left the port wing tip and went out to the horizon I noticed what appeared to be a long, low cloudbank stretching to the northeast as far as the eye could see.

At first I thought bad weather or ground fog might be moving in and then it dawned on me that I was looking at a huge body of water. The first thing that came to mind was Lake Winnipeg but a quick check with the map revealed that it was Lake Manitoba. It was like looking at the ocean because you certainly couldn't see the other side and apart from Lake Superior it was the largest body of fresh water that I had ever seen in my experience as a private pilot.

By now we were about 10 miles straight west of Portage La Prairie and it was just a matter of flying straight east along the highway until we reached it. We finally sighted the town, crossed over it and turned north just past the water tower gradually letting down. The ground elevation was only 860 feet here and we were starting to feel the effects of density altitude. My engine had always run rich and with more oxygen in the air it was performing better all the time.

We were now north of the town and spotted the field. It was beautiful green grass and the shorter mown grass of the runways was quite apparent. The Cub was turning final for runway 14 as I pulled on carb heat and reduced power. It was now 5:40 PM and the air quite smooth as I touched down on the loveliest grass runway I have ever landed on.

We taxied to the ramp that appeared to be quite deserted, parked and shut down. There was no one around but we found the Flying Club office open and went in and used the phone to close our flight plans. We now needed fuel for our takeoff early Sunday morning and after a short search found a list on the wall of five club members' names to call for fuel. I started down the list and had reached the fourth with no luck, which was not surprising for a Saturday night in July. There was one name left, Brian, and I noticed that the first three digits in his number were different from the others so I assumed he lived in a different part of town. I wondered if he was last on the list because he lived furthest away and I hesitated to call him.

We only needed five gallons of fuel each since we had come only 70 miles from Brandon and we might reach Pembina the next morning with fuel we had as it was about the same distance but we all agreed it would be preferable to leave with full tanks.

I crossed my fingers and dialed the last number, fortunately got an answer, and asked for Brain. I explained our problem and sure enough he lived furthest away but agreed to come even though he was going out for the evening. In about half an hour he arrived, was most cooperative and made us feel very welcome. We apologized for not buying more fuel and in order to help the Club out we rented hanger space for the night.

He was kind enough to drop us off at a hotel on the main street where we said goodnight and hoped we hadn't made him late for his evening out. We checked in and enjoyed the luxury of a hot shower and when I emerged there was a cold beer waiting. We lounged around while recounting the events of the day in a "debriefing" session and then decided it was time for a meal. We had apparently spent too long in our debriefing session for the dinner menu was no longer available but we were able to order a cold plate just before the dinning room closed.

On the subject of food, we reasoned that we would probably have difficulty getting an early breakfast on Sunday morning. We wanted to get in the air early as we would probably have delays clearing customs at Pembina.

Glen and I discovered a Dairy Queen close by so we bought some barbecued chicken burgers and put them away for breakfast.

Although we retired early it was not the most restful night as the band in the bar downstairs made up for in volume what they lacked in quality. However, my fatigue eventually won out and I awoke early Sunday morning feeling quite refreshed.

Somehow the barbecued chicken burgers that we had obtained at the D.Q. the night before had lost their appeal. They were cold, hard and dry with solidified grease in them. I had to force mine down and almost gagged several times in the process and once down my stomach was not particularly incline to keep it there.

We checked out and called a cab to take us to the airport which, fortunately, was not far away. As we were paying off the cab Glen realized that he didn't have his EAA jacket so the cab was dispatched back to the hotel to see if he left it in his room.

Meanwhile, we opened the hanger doors, rolled the aircraft out onto the apron and closed the doors again. We stowed our luggage aboard and did our walk around preflight inspections.

There is nothing as desolate as an airport with no one around, but this was a beautiful morning with sun low on the horizon shining on the grass and no sound except the odd bird. I finished polishing my windscreen, climb aboard and fastened my harness. Just then the cab appeared with Glen's jacket so all was ready. He swung my prop and the Continental came to life, ran rough for a few seconds, then settled down to its usual sound. The prop blades cast flickering shadows over the windscreen as the sun shone through them.

What little wind there was came from the south so we taxied out and backtracked along the length of runway 14 on which we had landed the night before, turned into the wind and shattered the silence of the morning with our runup. The grass rippled and flattened behind us, and the props threw up bits of grass and bugs mostly on the left side.

Back to the relative quiet of the idle, I released the brakes and watched the Cub turn onto runway 18, line up and begin to roll. The tail came up, the rudder waggled, the wheels left the ground and she seemed to go up like an elevator.

I always envied that climb. It had the same engine as mine but with a lower pitched prop and more wing area even with two people on board they could still out climb me. However, I have more forward speed and on a long cross-country this can help a lot. Because of this I waited a few moments before starting my takeoff roll and, due to the lower altitude, I was airborne sooner than usual. I noted the time off as 7:14 AM. I swung wide to the right to equalize our speeds, and then waited while I climbed up to their altitude and took up my position on their starboard quarter and a little below where I could keep them well in view and vice versa.

We had a good look at Portage as we crossed it and then headed southeast for the U.S. border and Pembina which lay just a mile or two beyond the border. We had phone ahead for customs clearance at Pembina and were told that a Customs Officer would be on hand to clear us into the U.S.

There were no outstanding landmarks on this leg so we had to pay close attention to our navigation and after about twenty minutes we ran through a band of light mist and fine drizzle. Moisture streaked in rivulets up the windscreen and I had to slide the canopy closed for about ten minutes as things were getting a bit damp.

As we approached Grand Forks I thought that I really should avoid flying over the densely populated area of the town. I started to turn to the east but realized that I would have to move to the other side of the Cub. As this would take me quite a bit off course I decided to go around the West Side of town.

Unfortunately, this brought me closer to the airport and Grand Forks is a major control zone. I turned my radio on but my 10 channel Radair did not have their frequency. I heard Glen asking me what I was doing and I replied that I was going around the west end of town. He said that the Tower wanted to know what was going on left me confused as I didn't realize that anything unusual was happening. I found out later that I was rather close to an airliner in the circuit for Grand Forks, which made me sweat a little, as I was totally unaware of its presence. I made a mental note to give control zones a wide berth in the future.

As what seemed like an eternity we eventually approached Fargo and called the Tower. We were cleared for a straight in approach and were advised to land short as military jets were using an intersecting runway near the south end.

At 1:00 PM we landed as short as we could and almost immediately stopped. I glanced at my airspeed indicator and thought there must be something wrong with it. It was reading 30 mph and flickering up to 35 and 40 and I wasn't even moving. No wonder it had taken so long to get there! Our ground speed must have been only about 30 to 40 mph. To make matters worse we still had to taxi about a mile and a half to the intersection. We could have made a normal approach and landed half way down the runway and still have had room to spare. Everything went smoothly until we turned off on the taxiway and then the fun began. The Cub was not supposed to be subjected to strong crosswinds and here we were in 30 mph. gusting to 40. Glen said later that he had Kay ready to get out and sit on the tail if need to be but somehow we made it into the ramp, parked and tied down as quickly as possible.

It was now 1:30 PM and with the wind that was blowing it was obvious that we would not be flying again for awhile. About this time as we were settling our fuel bill Glen nudged me and pointed out the window. There was an Airline Captain in uniform examining my Fly Baby so I went out and engaged him in conversation. He was very interested in homebuilt aircraft and asked me questions about my bird that I was delighted to answer. He was from Missouri and talked with an accent that was a little different from any southerner I had met before. Glen and Kay joined us and we got into a real hanger-flying session. He kept looking at his watch and several times said he should be going but he kept on telling us of his flying experiences.

Finally he tore himself away and ran for a 737 that was waiting on the ramp and we watched while he took off. That was one airline flight that was twenty minutes late but we felt good when we thought of how "grass roots" aviation can even be distracting to the "big boys".

We asked the ramp attendant when the wind was most likely to die down and he said that it never did. This was a bit of a shock to us as we didn't plan to remain in Fargo forever but we figured it was most likely to be calmest just about dawn so we planned to stay overnight and get an early start in the morning. Glen figured this would be a good time to work on his mag problem so after a pleasant lunch in the terminal he got out the tools and eventually solved the problem.

We were relieved to have that fixed as it was dangerous to leave an aircraft on the flight line with "hot mags" in the event that someone moved the prop.

We inquired about accommodations and the "Town House" was recommended as they also supplied transportation. The minibus from the hotel soon arrived for us and after a short drive we entered the lobby of the "Town House" to register. We noticed a large barrel of apples that said "Compliments of the Management" and I think Glen and I both got the same idea at the same time. Those apples would augment the airman's lunch tomorrow.

By the time we got checked in, showered and cleaned up it was just too late to get the dinner menu in the dining room so we had to settle for a cold plate again. This time we had them pack us a lunch for breakfast as we planned an early start and the dining room would not be open.

When we prepared for bed I looked out of the window and the flags were standing straight out and snapping so the wind was 20 mph plus.

At 5:30 AM they were still standing straight out but not snapping quite as loud so it seemed that our friend on the ramp was right. The wind never stops in Fargo, North Dakota.

Before leaving in the minibus we stocked up from the apple barrel in the lobby and then headed for the airport. When we arrived there at 6:00 AM the ramp gates were locked and the terminal was locked. We found a phone and called Flight Services and told them we would like a weather briefing and as they were on the second floor of the Terminal would they please come down and let us in. Soon a man appeared at the door and let us in and led us up to the weather office.

He was all alone and obviously welcomed company because we got the grand tour of the facilities and demonstrations of the equipment. I was particularly interested in a radarscope type machine that showed wind patterns over the whole continent. We could see how two systems from the east and west joined in the south to form a strong northerly flow up the middle of the continent. This accounted for the unusually strong southerly winds that we had encountered so far and which had given us all the problems with crosswind landing.

After our weather briefing we went down into the deserted waiting room to eat the breakfast we had brought with us. I found the food dry and I just couldn't force it down. I felt almost nauseated so finally gave up on it. This problem of feeding the inner man on a cross-country jaunt was getting serious.

Finally the security people arrived and we were allowed out on to the ramp to our aircraft. We did our pre-flight inspection carefully, untied the aircraft, filed our flight plan and fired up the engines.

The wind was still fairly brisk but had shifted a bit to the southeast. At least we had a runway directly into the wind so there was no crosswind factor this time.

After our runup and clearance from the Tower we took off at 6:30 AM, turned east and headed into the rising sun. Our destination was Little Falls, Minnesota so we headed generally southeast. The sun was just above the horizon and I was thinking to myself that this was really the most beautiful time of day. Everything was running smoothly and I was really enjoying myself. I glanced out at the port wing and did a double take. The fabric on the upper surface had wrinkles on it! My mind went into high gear and icy fingers of fear clutched my heart. What could cause the fabric to wrinkle? There were no tears or obvious signs of damage. If the upper surface was wrinkled the wing must be flexing upward. Was I experiencing a spar failure? What action should I take? I kept watching it and it didn't seem to get any worse. I looked over at the right wing. No problem there! The longer I looked at the offending surface the less it seemed to be wrinkled and finally it disappeared. I finally concluded that the low angle of the sun on the horizon had created an optical illusion of some sort.

Finally my heartbeat returned to normal and anxiety faded. We were now approaching Detroit Lakes, which was on our left. I recalled passing through this town in the Greyhound bus thirty years ago and the peculiar name stuck in my head. We were in Minnesota now which is noted for its many lakes and we were crossing a large group of these now. The beauty of the sunrise reflecting like liquid gold on these multiple lakes was breathtaking. This is something that only the airmen can see as it is lost to view on the ground.

The lakes became green farmland and eventually we reached Little Falls. There was a nice paved strip and here we made a straight in approach from the northwest. As we taxied into the fuel pumps at 8:30 AM we realized that the ramp and taxiway had just been oiled or tarred.

We had no choice but to walk through the gooey mess to get to the pumps. A man and woman came out to help us and were very apologetic for the fresh oil and gave us the royal treatment to make up for the inconvenience. When we had refueled we pushed the aircraft back into the grass to avoid having to taxi through it again. By doing this we had to walk through it again to get to the office and I am sure I was three inches taller from the build up of tar and pebbles on the soles of my brand new jogging shoes.

We noticed a sign saying that it was Charles Lindbergh's hometown so we felt that this was a rather special occasion. We had a coffee break, bought some charts and planned the next leg of our trip. We decided to stay well north of the high-density area of Minneapolis—St. Paul and picked Amery as our next stop, ten miles into the state of Wisconsin. This would be a shorter hop of about 110 miles.

As the wind was still from the south we asked the F.B.O. if we could take off from the grass instead of a crosswind takeoff on the pavement. He said it would be O.K. but to watch for a big cross made of snow fencing in the middle of the runway about halfway down. After filing our flight plan for Amery we had to cross the wet tar again to get to the aircraft. I tried to scrape as much off as I could but my shoes were a real mess. We taxied out across the grass rather than use the newly tarred taxiway and turned right along the main runway.

We found the grass strip running perpendicular to the paved strip, turned left on it, set the brakes, and did our runup. I could not see the snow fence marker but decided to stay on the right side of the strip to avoid it.

When the Cub was airborne and climbing I advanced the throttle and started my take off roll. Stick ahead to get the nose up! Forty, fifty mph. Where was the marker? I didn't want to hit it at this speed. Sixty, sixty-five and back on the stick. Still no sign of the marker. Oh well! I was 100 feet above it now anyway. It must have been beneath my port wing. Later I compared notes with Glen and Kay and they hadn't seen it either so we never did find out if it was there.

The flight to Amery was mostly over green farmland so we had to watch our navigation, as there were few distinct landmarks. After about an hour we passed Cambridge and saw its airstrip on our right. About 30 minutes later Amery came into view. Its airstrip should be southeast of the town. Then I saw it about halfway up a hillside. There was a steep drop of about 50 to 100 feet at the north end over which we would have to approach and the hill rose again to the southeast. It was almost like a shelf on a wall but I guess the mind makes some funny comparisons. We flew over the town and approached the cliff. Be ready for down drafts! Everything smooth so far. The Cub was down and taxiing back on the grass to my left as I settled in and made reasonably gentle contact with the ground. I punched in the carb heat button, swung left onto the grass and we taxied up to the pumps. It was now 11:30 AM.

There didn't seem to be anybody around so we figured the attendant was out to lunch somewhere. We walked into the office and found a phone on the wall so the first order of business was to close our flight plans, which had to be done through Minneapolis flight control.

Kay put a quarter in the phone and that was the first of a series of problems. We had only been in the country twenty-four hours and had used our credit cards for all transactions so nobody had any American coins and that telephone wasn't accepting any Canadian quarters. We next tried the toll free zenith number to use for closing flight plans but the operator would not accept it because it was across a state line in Minnesota and we were now in Wisconsin. After some discussion Glen and Kay remembered that they had a telephone calling card so the call finally went through and we were able to close the flight plan.

The next problem was to get some fuel. The only signs of life were two men working on a racing car in one of the back hangers. We asked about fuel and they thought the attendant had probably gone home for lunch and they gave me the home phone number. They were also kind enough to let me use their phone so I didn't have a coin problem. When I finally got through I was told that he was out of town and would not be back until the following day.

We went back and took a look at the fuel pumps. They seemed to be a type of self-serve pump in which a number combination was entered. I presume the locals all had their own numbers and helped themselves and then paid up at the end of the month, which didn't do a thing towards solving our problem. We had visions of a half-mile hike into town to buy automotive gas and a long trek back with jerry cans and maybe several trips if we had to carry it.

We went back to where the men were working on the racecar and explained our problem. One of them said he would phone his boss as he had a light twin for his business and his own personal supply of 100-octane aviation fuel. When he got his boss on the line he let me talk to him. I explained the situation and he agreed to sell us some of his fuel. He said that he was not supposed to but as this was an emergency he would help out. I thanked him profusely and then he asked to talk to his man again and told him to co-operate with us. Hundred octane was a little potent for our engines but we weren't about to quibble at the point.

We went back to the airplanes and started our engines and taxied around the first row of hangers and along a long taxi strip to last hanger in the second row and shut down again. The gas pump did not have a meter but a bell rang with every gallon pumped through. We counted the rings and made it come out even so we would not have a problem with change.

The race car mechanics became very interested in my custom-built aircraft. This was something they understood since they were working on a custom-built car.

We were now refueled. At least the aircraft were. We had no coins to fit the vending machines in the office so we had to settle for the apples from the Town House in Fargo.

We plotted a course for Wisconsin Rapids, filed a flight plan, and started up. The takeoff at 1:30 PM was uneventful and we climbed out to the south and then turned around the hill to the east. The countryside was becoming less open and more densely covered with trees. The open areas seemed to have been cleared for cultivation. The fewer choices one has to make a forced landing the more conscious one becomes of this situation. I found myself looking for alternate landing spots and trying to be prepared. In spite of this I was quite enjoying myself. The day was beautiful. Hot sunshine poured down on us and the beautiful green forests and fields of Wisconsin stretched out below us.

Fifty-five miles later we passed over Chippewa Falls on the Flambeau Rive just northeast of Eau Claire and the forest was becoming a little denser and fewer open spaces were in sight. About 2:45 PM we spotted the Wisconsin River which runs north out of Petenwell Lake. The town of Wisconsin was on the east bank. We flew across the river and over town towards the airstrip just south of town. There was quite a bit of industrial smoke from the town, which I took to be wood smoke, probably from a lumber or pulp mill. The direction of the smoke indicated that the wind was still from the south so a straight-in approach would be the order of the day. It was a beautiful, long, wide, paved strip with a thick growth of trees along the west side so that by the time we were below tree level there was virtually no wind. Our landings were nothing to be ashamed of. In fact, with all the practice we had had we were getting pretty good at it. I had put in more hours in the last three days than I normally would in a season.

We taxied ahead to the intersection, turned left and in towards the terminal and the ramp. I was impressed with this airport as it appeared clean and tidy and well maintained. The ramp service was quick and efficient and we were soon refueled and ready. We were only about an hour's flying time from Oshkosh now and the excitement was starting to mount. We checked the time. It was a little after 3:30 PM. We knew that Oshkosh was closed from 4:00PM to 7:00 PM each day for the airshow so we would not make it in time so we decided to go into town and have a leisurely meal and then continue on to Oshkosh after the airshow.

We were shown a place where we could park and tie down and the manager offered us a ride into town as he was going that way. We enjoyed the ride and the scenery with all the trees around. He dropped us off at a motel with a nice restaurant and lounge and we went into the dining room. For once we were early for dinner and realized we had not had a good, hot dinner since we left home. Airport lunchrooms were few and far between and had very little in the way of good, substantial food. We took our time and enjoyed our meal and then started to walk back to the airport. Although a lot of it was rural we passed quite a few nice residences and the whole area gave the impression of being neat and well kept.

We eventually arrived back at the airport and as we still had lots of time we indulged in a tour of the local T-hangers and private aircraft. Again everything seemed to be clean and neat. This must be prosperous area as we didn't see any peeling paint or anything in a poor state of repair and the grass was all neatly trimmed. I decided I would like to live in this area and fly from a field like this. In Canada we seem to have either large, high-density centers with control zones, ATC and radar or marginal operations where there is perhaps interest but lack of volume, money and/or population to create a situation such as we now saw before us.

The time for departure eventually rolled around so we untied and did our pre-flight inspections. The last time I flew into Oshkosh was on a Saturday night after the airshow four years before. I was in the back seat of a friend's Beech Staggerwing and as I looked out of the window all I could see was props, tail wheels, wing tips and landing gear surrounding us in all directions. In all a very tense situation.

We phoned in our flight plan and got the procedure all straightened out in our minds. This was the final leg and we were getting all psyched up for the flight into high-density traffic and precision flying.

I climbed aboard, put on my brain bucket and strapped in. Glen swung the prop and it became a blur. I sat there warming up while he went over and propped the Cub with Kay at the controls in the front seat. His engine was now running and he climbed into the rear seat, strapped in and put on his head set. Finally the Cub moved out of the line of parked aircraft , swung right and on to the taxiway. I gave the throttle a nudge and released the brakes and fell in line behind him. At the intersection we turned right and backtracked to the north end of the runway. There was a hard-surfaced area on the east side of the runway and we pulled off into this to do our runups.

Everything checked out and the Cub moved out, lined up and started to roll. I checked the approach. All clear. I moved out, lined up and opened the throttle. The tail came up and I held her steady down the white line. Rotate. We were off and climbing. As soon as we cleared the trees at the south end we found ourselves out over the waters of Petenwell Lake. It came as a surprise because on the ground it was completely hidden by the trees. We turned left towards Oshkosh. The Cub was above me with the evening sun lighting up its yellow paint job. The air was smooth as silk. A beautiful evening for flying! Stay alert and be mentally sharp. This is it! We are going to tangle with all the aircraft converging on Oshkosh.

Wait a minute! What was going on here? The Cub was turning left and descending. I followed puzzled. I tried to get Glen on the radio but no answer. Something was amiss! I resigned myself to follow him as we were doing this together. We were now in the circuit and over the town. The air was cooler and very pleasant. The Cub was on final, over the trees, down and rolling.

I followed in taking my time. In this smooth air everything was going beautifully. I was sinking toward the runway in the shadow of the evergreen stand on my right. Lower and lower. I didn't feel the wheels touch but I heard the tires chirp. Back on the throttle, slightly ahead with the stick to pin her down for the most perfect landing I have ever made and won't you know it, not a soul watching. The tail eventually dropped to the runway and I rolled towards the intersection. Card heat off and I taxied back to the parking space that I had just left and shut down. Glen was out and walking towards me with an unhappy look on his face.

I pulled off my helmet so I could hear and asked him what the problem was. It seemed that his radio was dead. The batteries had run down during the day and there was not enough power left to operate the radio.

It was at times like this that I was glad that I had installed a solar charger panel to charge my battery. I was using a lead-acid motorcycle battery and the solar charger had kept the charge up all the way so far. Of course I had only used the radio in control zones or at pre-arranged times when we had agreed to communicate.

We accepted our fate and agreed that we should stay overnight in Wisconsin Rapids and recharge his batteries at the same time. I felt a little relieved at this as we could make a fresh start in the early morning when there would probably be less traffic and the light would be better. All of these were rationalizations in my mind of course for putting off the moment of mixing it up with a lot of other aircraft in the circuit over Oshkosh.

We pushed the aircraft into tie-down area, secured them, and took out our overnight bags. While we were doing this a man and woman came up and started talking to us. When they learned of our predicament they offered us a ride into town which we gratefully accepted. This was the second time that day that this had happened and I was beginning to be quite favorably impressed by the local hospitality.

Finally we were ready and we were still standing there talking to the woman. After awhile we asked her where her husband had gone and she replied that he had gone home to get the car. We were a little taken aback by this and asked how they had gotten to the airport. It turned out that they had a Cessna 150 and had ridden out on their motorcycle to pay their parking fees.

We had a hard time believing that he would go to all the trouble of riding home on the motorbike to get the car just to give us a ride to town.

He finally showed up in a robin-egg blue Cadillac. Not one of the new, small Cadillacs but one of the older big, long limousines. They introduced themselves as Don and Julie Rucks and we put our bags in the trunk, climbed in and settled back to enjoy this luxury.

On the way to town Don turned and asked us if we would do them the honor of coming the their house and having a drink with them. The honor! We felt we were the ones being honored with this treatment. Not having any other plans we accepted with thanks. Their home faced the river separated only by a road so it was a very pleasant outlook.

As if sensing our desire to secure accommodations, Julie got on the phone and made reservations for us at a motel.

Don asked us what we would like to drink and I replied that I would take whatever he had but he insisted that I state my preference so I said that I would like a rum and coke. A few minutes later I saw him go out to his car and drive off. I felt really embarrassed as it was obvious that he was going out to buy coke and perhaps even rum.

We spent a very pleasant evening with them and Don showed us a new portable radio he had just purchased for a backup radio in his Cessna 150. The first thing he had heard on it was Dick Rutan talking to Oshkosh Tower from the Voyager and he was quite excited about that. Apparently Dick was in the process of transferring fuel from one tank to another to get the aircraft's balance just right prior to landing at Oshkosh.

Julie told us that she was going to have her first flying lesson at 11:30 the next morning and she was having some preflight butterflies in the stomach at the thought. We assured her that she would probably do very well and hoped they would have many enjoyable hours in their 150.

It finally came time to go and they drove us to our motel, which happened to be the same place that we had had dinner earlier. They insisted on picking us up in the morning for breakfast at their house and then driving us to the airport. The hospitality was completely overwhelming and I had to ask myself if I would do the same for complete strangers in my country. I resolved that in the future I would make the effort.

Our quarters were quite comfortable and after making sure that Glen's battery charger was plugged into the wall socket we turned in for the night.

The next morning we were up bright and early. As I came out of the shower Glen was watching the weather forecast on TV. It looked like a good flying day and I felt in much better shape to tackle the flight into Oshkosh. By the time we checked out Julie was there in the big, blue Cadillac to drive us to the house.

I kidded her about Don sleeping in and sending her to chauffeur us but she said that he was busy making breakfast. He was, too, and it was some breakfast. Bacon and eggs and hot cakes filled us up to the point where I was sure I was going to need more than the usual takeoff run to get off the ground.

Don had to be at work at 8:00 AM so he wished us a good flight and left on the motorbike. Julie dropped us off at the airport where we said goodbye, thanked her for their kind hospitality, and wished her luck on her flying lesson.

It was a beautiful day and we looked forward to arriving at Oshkosh. We went through the procedure of getting the aircraft ready, flight planning and taxiing out to the end of the runway and had, in fact, finished our runup. I looked over at Glen expecting him to move into position for takeoff but he just sat there. I pointed to my microphone indicating that I wanted to talk to him but he just shook his head and started to taxi back to the ramp. I followed, not knowing what was occurring but I was sure I was about to find out.

We returned to our parking stops and shut down. He climbed out and walked over to me with an unhappy expression on his face saying that he could kick himself. It turned out that the wall outlet he had been using to charge his batteries in the motel had been on the TV outlet which was connected to a switch on the wall. It had been turned off all night and the only time his batteries had been charging was when he was watching the weather forecast on TV that morning.

We were now in the same situation as the night before so we figured that only solution was to replace the NiCad rechargeable batteries in his radio with AA Alkaline flashlight batteries. As long as they lasted for an hour that would get us to Oshkosh. As the flashlight batteries were a slightly different voltage he would need an extra one and, being an electrician, he had all this figured out.

We now needed to get back to town to buy batteries. All this discussion had taken place in the waiting room of the flight office and the lady at the counter came forward dangling a set of keys and offered her car for the trip. It turned out to be a brand new car and I couldn't believe that some-one would do this for perfect strangers. Fate certainly seemed to be on our side so off we went. We soon found a shopping center and a hardware store. While Glen was stocking up on batteries I got some quick-driving epoxy and tape in case I had to make some more prop repairs. Back at the airport Glen was able to borrow a soldering gun and solder the ten batteries together. We finally tested it and it looked like we were back in business.

We got Oshkosh on the phone and filed our flight plan. I told them that I did not have the ATIS frequency and the controller told me that I could not fly without prior written permission. This was a setback so I explained that I did not have the Approach frequency and the Tower frequency so he relented and told me to fly tight formation with the Cub, dead astern and slightly below and they would bring us in together. As we were climbing into our aircraft I half expected to see Julie show up for her lesson as it was about that time. Once more we taxied out and I couldn't help thinking how kind the citizens of Wisconsin Rapids had been to us.

We did our runup and took off at 12:25 PM over the lake and swung to the left heading for Oshkosh. We were finally on our last leg of the journey.

The big moment was at hand! The sun was shining and at that time it was high in the sky and not in our eyes as it would have been earlier. However, the traffic was probably getting thicker and I wasn't too happy about that. I hoped Glen was listening to the ATIS (Air Traffic Information Service) frequency and getting all the necessary information which reminded me to tune in on the Approach frequency. I listened but could not pick up anything so I shut the set off again. No point in running the battery down as I would certainly need it later. After about half an hour's flying time we saw the west arm of Lake Winnebago in the distance and we turned south towards Ripon. I fell in behind and below the Cub as much as I dared according to the controller's instructions. Soon we had Rush Lake coming up on our left and I went over the published sequence in my mind. Follow the railway line northeast from Ripon to Fisk and if the approach control at Fisk does not acknowledge your existence, make a left hand circuit around Rush Lake back to Ripon and start over again until you get the go-ahead to continue. I turned my radio on again to receive transmissions from Approach Control as we were almost at Ripon but all I could hear was hash and the arcs from my spark plugs. We had passed Ripon and I expected we would be turning up the railway but we kept on going in a southeasterly direction. This wasn't what I was expecting but Glen had more frequencies than I did so I assumed that he knew something that I didn't. I still hadn't heard anything on the Approach Frequency so I thought we should be circling the lake, which was far behind us now. On we went and I really couldn't tell where we were as I was concentrating hard on holding my position in relation to the Cub.

I looked out to the starboard and just ahead I could see an airport. My first thought was that we had overshot and gone down to Fond du Lac. As we got closer I could spot familiar landmarks. This was Wittman Field! We had arrived! I quickly switched to Tower frequency and now I started to hear transmissions. They were talking to us. Join the circuit to the north of the field, swing east over Lake Winnebago and approach heading west.

Where was all the traffic I had expected? I was all keyed up for this and looked all around and as near as I could see we were the only two aircraft in the circuit. What a relief! No high-density problems! Everybody must have been down for lunch! We were now flying east along the north side of the field and the Tower was very helpful giving us instructions. Now we were over the lake and turning south on our base leg. I had never been over such a large body of water before and it gave me quite an eerie feeling but you do what you have to do. The Controller's reassuring voice came in once again telling us to turn on final. Glen was instructed to land long and began his approach. About this time a light twin approached from the south dead ahead of me but lower and, being faster, turned in under and ahead of me. I stayed high to give us enough separation. He was instructed to land halfway down the runway. The Tower was now instructing me to land on the number and as I was now higher than I would have been if the twin had not got in between us I had to dive pretty steeply to put her on the button. As a result my speed was a little excessive and when I touched down I was not fast enough getting the stick ahead to keep her pinned down. I was flying again. Once more she settled. Just a little bounce this time and then I was down and rolling. Wouldn't you know it? Last night I made the perfect landing with no one to see it and today with the whole aviation fraternity watching I had to bounce twice.

Oh well! They say that any landing that you can walk away from is a good one. I was soon distracted by the activity all around me. A man off the runway to my right was holding a sign towards me. What does it say? Camping? No. I shook my head. He pointed to my left. Another man was beckoning me off the runway. I turned left onto the grass. A boy on a motorbike with a sign "Follow Me" swung in front of me and I gave the throttle a burst of power and followed. I didn't see any sign of the Cub but they had landed long so would probably be coming shortly. We moved past row after row of aircraft and I kept weaving to see ahead. There was activity everywhere. Props turning, aircraft taxiing, flags fluttering, people waving. I waved back. This was just like winning the Grand Prix! All those years of work building, the hours of test flying and accumulating flying hours, the flight to get here all culminated in this moment and made it worth while. There was a tremendous feeling of excitement and exhilaration. A real high!

After what seemed like miles of taxiing the motorbike turned off to the right and the right again. This was my parking space. He waved and was off. I looked to my right and saw that I was parked right beside a VariEze. Talk about the old and the new! My Fly Baby looked like the Wright Flyer beside that machine.

As soon as I shut down I was surrounded by people asking questions. "Did you build it yourself?" "What is it made of?" "How much did it cost?" "How long did it take to build?"

While glorying in all this attention I was conscious of attending to the business of closing the flight plan etc. I had seen the Cub taxiing by to the Antique and Classic area, so reluctantly I excused myself and ran over to join them. It seems that their engine had stopped on the landing rollout so they had to restart and that was what had caused the delay. We were now at a much lower altitude and his carburetor was set too lean. This worked out fine for me as my engine had always run far too rich, in spite of everything I had done to adjust it, and so it was now in its element.

Kay and I soon located some pay phones and closed the flight plans. Now we could relax and enjoy the Convention. We went over to the Antique and Classic headquarters which was in a larger trailer. There we met George Lemay and his daughter, Jean, from Calgary who were on duty, George York from Tullahoma, Tennessee, Jim Mankins from California and other old friends from previous conventions of aircraft buffs. They offered us cool drinks and while we were relating some of the adventures of our trip I suddenly realized that in all the excitement I had not tied the airplane down. I knew that they were quite emphatic about tie-downs so I dashed off to attend to this important duty. I reached the aircraft and dug my tie-downs out of the baggage compartment and was down on my hands and knees in the process of securing the wings when a pretty young lady official came along and thanked me profusely for tying down saying how much they appreciated it. I was too embarrassed to admit that I had forgotten and gave her a sheepish grin as if I knew what I was doing all along. I suspect that she had noticed earlier that it was untied and so I wasn't really fooling anybody. At any rate she was very diplomatic about it and this is typical of the whole operation. Everyone cooperates and if you do slip up they ask for your cooperation in a way to which no one can take exception. The grounds are clean. Everyone puts their refuse in the many containers that are provided and the volunteer organization is really to be complimented.

With these duties now fulfilled I racked my brain to think of anything else I had overlooked and as I couldn't think of any I went back to join the gang but shortly they had to go back to work judging vintage aircraft.

Glen and I wandered over to the registration booth to sign in and were presented with pilot's coffee cups with the EAA crest on them. I was delighted with mine and it is still my favorite coffee cup. I don't know who thought up the idea but it was certainly a nice, welcome touch.

I had been to Oshkosh twice before but this was the first time I had flown my own ship in and it was quite a different feeling.

The convention was very enjoyable and we spent the rest of the week looking at aircraft, attending forums, enjoying the daily airshows and hanger flying with friends.

I discovered another Fly Baby driver and compared notes with him and as far as I know we had the only two Fly Babys there at that time. He told me that he had pre-authorization to come in Nordo (no radio) and that it had worked very well. It might save a lot of problems with no radio equipment but it is rather reassuring to have the Controller's voice guiding you and making you aware of other traffic that you might not otherwise see.

The only thing I had a problem with was the heat and humidity and the lower altitude. By the end of the day my feet were burning and I felt exhausted but there was still more to be seen. I think if a person stayed there a month they still would not be able to take it all in. One just has to establish priorities and stick to them.

Saturday finally arrived and it was time to leave. It was rather sad to see everyone departing and things closing down but all good things must come to an end.

We started to plan our trip back and, as the Cub had originally come from the Nebraska area, Glen and Kay wanted to go back that way and perhaps look up some of the previous owners. It had changed hands many times and of course the owner's name appeared in the logbooks. This was all right of them as they were flying a certified aircraft but I had to get prior FAA approval for border crossing and the letter stated that I should proceed to the Convention and return by the most direct and practicable route.

The route back across Iowa to Nebraska was slightly out of the way but not that much. I was mainly concerned as to whether or not border crossing should be at a specific place or more particularly whether I must return the way I had come. As the FAA (Federal Aviation Authority) had an office at Oshkosh and, indeed, we had to attend a pilot's briefing held by the FAA before we left, I thought I would check it out there.

The gentleman that I talked to was quite cooperative and said that he could see no reason why I couldn't return any way that I wanted. In fact he pointed out that the visibility was so bad to the northwest which is the way we had come that we could only get a VFR (Visual Flight Rules) clearance to the south or southwest. This would comply with my letter as being the most practicable route.

Having that matter out of the way we decided on Madison, the capital of Wisconsin, as our first stop. It would serve as both a lunch and fuel stop.

All VFR flights had been delayed due to poor visibility and we had to wait until nearly noon before we could leave. We attended the pilot's briefing and the FAA man outlined the procedure. We were to taxi to the runway and line up in pairs and the controller on the runway would wave us off at his discretion. We were given yellow cards to show that we had attended the briefing and we had to hold these up to the controller before we were allowed on the runway.

We finally got VFR clearance but were told that we must stay below 500 feet and continue to the south end of Lake Winnebago before making any course changes. No one was allowed to go north, east or west.

We climbed aboard, started up and joined the line of aircraft taxiing out to the north end of the long north-south runway. We held up our yellow cards and were directed onto the runway. We were side by side with me on the left and Glen and Kay on the right. We had done our runups and were ready to take off. It reminded me of a drag race. The controller was standing between us and out in front. He suddenly pointed at the Cub and waved it off. As soon as it left the ground he pointed at me and waved me off. This was a very efficient system and it worked beautifully. Aircraft were leaving about every 30 seconds.

We were now off and climbing at 11:40 AM. From the ground things didn't look too bad but now we could see that the situation wasn't that great. Smog lay in the banks all around us and even at 500 feet the ground was rather hazy. We knew that we were in a stream of aircraft heading south but we couldn't see them. It was hard to see each other. After about 30 miles of this we reached the end of the lake and started to alter course to the southwest for Madison.

A short time later I glanced down to the right to see a radio or TV tower reaching out of the smog almost to my altitude. This was getting downright dangerous!

As we proceeded the visibility gradually began to improve, presumably because we were getting further away from Lake Winnebago and Lake Michigan.

After about an hour and a half in the air Madison appeared out of the haze. The airport was northeast of the city so we reached it first. The tower gave us runway 18 so with a slight swing to the right we were cleared for a straight—in approach.

Great, wide runways stretched forever so this time we landed long, close to the intersection to avoid miles of taxiing. I had landed here four years before and couldn't see anything that even resembled what I had remembered but I turned east at the intersection and headed for what appeared to be gas pumps and a ramp. When arriving there seemed to be a choice so I waited for the Cub to show up. For some reason we had gotten separated and it was quite awhile before they showed up. I sat there waiting with my engines running as I was not sure where they were and there were some buildings in the way so I could not see the taxiway. The heat was getting unbearable and my oil temperature was getting close to the red line. I didn't want to shut the engine off in case I had to move and a single-handed hot start was something I didn't relish. Finally they appeared around the corner of the building and when they had parked beside me we both shut down. It was a relief to get inside the nice, air-conditioned building and we had a late lunch an planned the next leg of the trip. We first thought of Cedar Rapids, Iowa, and then I thought I would like to see Davenport again as I had lived there for three years while attending the Palmer College of Chiropractic. It was a distance of about 130 miles or close to two hours of flying time at our speed and although it was closer than Cedar Rapids it was further south.

After servicing the aircraft we fired up and taxied out and did our runups. We would be taking off to the west this time which was the direction we were heading anyway.

Glen got a takeoff clearance and then an airliner was moving into position so I hesitated. The Tower called me and said if I wanted to join my buddy to go ahead. I smiled at the informality and took off. Although the visibility was still a little hazy it was a vast improvement over our trip from Oshkosh. At least there were no unpleasant surprises lurking in the mist like TV towers and tall stacks that we couldn't see.

The countryside was very green presumably because of the high humidity and there were no major landmarks until we crossed the Mississippi at Savanna. I was surprised at the amount of shipping and boat traffic and marine craft tied up at the docks. The river is quite wide with several islands at this point and made for interesting viewing.

Shortly afterwards we passed Clinton, Iowa, which I remembered from having attended an airshow there in 1957.

Davenport soon came into view and we circled to the northwest and landed on runway 13 at 4:50 PM. We taxied into a very nice terminal building and, after refueling, pushed the aircraft onto a beautiful well-kept green grass area and tied down.

Glen and Kay wandered over to the edge of the field and surveyed a corn crop. Iowa is famous for its corn, which is used mainly for livestock feed, and this crop stood nearly 14 feet high. This was nothing to me as I had lived in this area for three years but Glen had been observing these beautiful green areas as possible emergency landing fields and when he saw at close quarters what he would have forced landed in he felt a little sick.

The heat was really oppressive here and we phoned to a motel with a pick-up service and soon the minibus arrived for us. The motel was air-conditioned and had an indoor swimming pool so after checking in we had a nice cooling swim in the pool, a nice cool drink in the bar and a lovely buffet dinner in the dining room.

I tried phoning old contacts but they had either moved away or did not answer. We had no transportation and the motel was closer to the airport than the town. I didn't fancy venturing forth into that oppressive heat again so having had a long day we retired at a reasonable hour to be fresh for Sunday.

We were up bright and early, had a good breakfast in the dining room, checked out and requested the courtesy bus to the airport. The regular driver was occupied elsewhere at the moment so a middle-aged chamber-maid that was just coming into work was pressed into service.

We had our first doubts as to her driving ability when she had difficulty finding where to put the ignition key. She was a jolly, cheerful soul and said she hoped it was an automatic as she couldn't drive a standard shift.

She was delighted to find it was an automatic and got it started. After a couple of near misses in the parking lot she got it out onto the highway and seemed to have some difficulty staying on the right side of the centerline. Fortunately there was not much traffic early Sunday morning. We came to a major intersection of highways and the traffic light was suspended in the center and fairly high. The light was red and I am sure she didn't even see the signal for she drove right through without even slowing down. We all looked at each other and silently thanked our lucky stars there had been no traffic coming the other road.

We reached the airport in one piece and thankfully climbed out and with a cheery wave she was off again. I still wonder if she made it back to the motel. A friend of mine once said that the most dangerous part of flying was driving to and from the airport and it certainly seemed to hold true that day.

Although it was only 10:30 AM it was already hot and sticky and promised to get worse as the day wore on. I looked forward to getting into the air where I could fly open cockpit with the breeze in my face.

We untied the aircraft and did our preflight inspections and then went back into the air-conditioned office to plot our first leg of the day. We chose Knoxville, Iowa, as our first stop as it was fairly direct and made a trip of about 135 miles or so which would be a little over two hours flying time, about optimum for an enjoyable flight.

We had the whole airport to ourselves so takeoff was no problem and once en route the air stream was relatively cool compared to the ground. The temperature was in the 90's Fahrenheit, however, and I noticed the oil temperature creeping up towards the red line. My tar-stained jogging shoes were unbearably hot even without socks but I didn't think I wanted to fly barefoot.

After crossing the Des Moines River we landed at Knoxville at 12:30 and serviced the aircraft. We looked around the terminal for food but all I could see was vending machines. One machine had sandwiches and I was about to try it when Glen came and said we were going into town for lunch.

We I asked how we were going to get there the lady behind the desk handed me her car keys and gave us directions to one or two restaurants. She had parked her car in the hanger to keep it out of the sun and it certainly made a difference. It was a brand new Pontiac diesel and was quite a treat to drive. We were getting used to this courtesy car treatment and decided to enjoy it because it would change as soon as we crossed the border back into Canada.

We found a nice, clean, air-conditioned restaurant and enjoyed a leisurely lunch. I guess we were putting off the moment that we would have to venture forth into that stifling, humid heat again. It might be a good climate for growing Iowa corn but it is tough on Canadians who are used to higher and drier air.

We finally drove back to the airport and got the maps out to plan the next stop. Glen and Kay wanted to look up former owners of the Cub in the Omaha area but as this was a high density area we decided on Council Bluffs, Iowa which is just across the Missouri River from Omaha.

We taxied out to the end of runway 13 and couldn't see anything but high corn crops on all sides. We took off and after a right turn out set course for Council Bluffs 150 miles away.

There was nothing outstanding about the Iowa countryside, just green corn but the heat was almost unbearable. The air was heavy and humid and sat like a lead weight on your chest. It was almost difficult to breathe. The visibility was not good enough to fly more than 2000 feet above the ground. We could not fly high enough to get into cooler air and so we just had to stay low and sweat it out.

I had the canopy fully opened as I had for all the trip so far but just could not get any relief. I was conscious of the hot engine just on the other side of the firewall throwing blast furnace heat on my feet. If I lived in this part of the world I would put some fresh air vents in the fuselage to blow on my feet. Of course I had the wrong shoes on for this kind of weather but even without socks they were far too hot. In retrospect I suppose I should have brought a cooler pair of shoes as well but I was very limited for space and size 13's take up a lot of room.

I watched the oil temperature creep up to just under the red line at 220 degrees Fahrenheit and wondered if the engine was going to suffer as a result but that little Continental just droned on and on and never missed a beat. Developing quite an affection for it and hated to see it taking this kind of abuse.

We were about 50 miles out of Council Bluffs when I glanced out past the starboard wing tip and saw strobe lights flashing in the haze. It gave me a bit of a jolt as they seemed to be almost at my altitude. I checked the map and saw that we were flying over an area containing a group of six radio or TV towers, the highest of which was 1507 feet above ground. We had plenty of height over the others but this one was getting too close for comfort! Fortunately our track was a mile or so south of this monster but it made me aware of the fact that no matter how carefully you plan you can also overlook something.

The great sprawling mass of the combination of Council Bluffs and Omaha soon appeared but the Council Bluffs airstrip was east of the town so we reached it first.

We let down and swung in a wide left turn to approach from the north. Council Bluffs is on high ground overlooking the Missouri River to the west, which is also the state line between Iowa and Nebraska. The airstrip was southeast of the town on an even higher plateau. It was a nice little single strip running north and south in a wooded area and though it was now 4:50 PM it was still blistering hot. We had to get into the relative comfort of the air-conditioned office several times during the servicing of the aircraft and by the time this was done and they were tied down for the night we were exhausted and wringing wet.

We now needed a ride to town and one of the local private pilots offered us a ride. His car was in the parking lot with the engine and air-condition on and he was waiting for it to cool off enough to drive.

Ken Burch and his wife, Jane, ran the operation. They were very pleasant and while we were waiting Jane showed me a Luscombe Silvaire that they had bought and were restoring.

The aluminum skin was pitted and rough and they had been hand polishing it back into condition. I couldn't see myself hand polishing anything in that heat but I guess you adapt to the climate you live in. Maybe they have some cool days in the spring and fall.

We got our lift into town when the car had cooled off and the gentleman dropped us off at a nice air-conditioned motel. After checking into our room we decided what we needed first was a cold drink so we went into the bar and there sat the man who had driven us to town so we were able to show our appreciation by buying a couple of rounds. I don't think I have ever appreciated a cold beer more than I did that night.

We then had a refreshing shower and by this time felt civilized enough to go down to the dining room for a good steak.

It was still too hot to go outside and the motel was not exactly downtown so we didn't see much of Council Bluffs.

Glen phone some of the Cub's previous owners and one old chap in his eighties was interested but he had just returned from a family reunion and didn't feel that he had the strength to go out again.

Another family in Yankton, South Dakota, were quite interested although this was the son of a previous owner and not a pilot himself. He agreed to meet us in Yankton for lunch the following day so that determined our first stop.

Even though we were up in good time, by the time we had breakfast and took a taxi to the airport it was after 9:00 AM. We plotted our course, filed our flight plans and did our preflight inspections. It was uncomfortably hot already but from here we would be heading north so perhaps we could be getting into a cooler climate. We watched an ultra-light take off and fly around. I wondered if he was any cooler sitting out exposed to the breeze. At 9:45 AM we started up and began to taxi out. Jane came out and gave us a friendly wave goodbye.

We had to back track to the north end of the runway as the wind was from the south. We took off and set course for Yankton. We flew to the north of Omaha to avoid the high-density area and headed about 325 degrees magnetic or generally northwest. In the first twenty minutes we crossed the Missouri River three times as our course took us over its bends. We soon found ourselves over the open country of Nebraska while the Missouri River was now far off to our right. We passed over Tekemah, Lyons, Emerson and Wakefield and at this point we could see the faint outline of Sioux City, Iowa, on the Missouri on the eastern horizon.

As we droned on and on the Missouri came back from the right to meet us until it lay right across our path with Yankton on the opposite shore. As the Missouri is also the state line, when we crossed it we passed from Nebraska into South Dakota. We flew past the east edge of Yankton and landed on the airport just north of town.

As I climbed out of the airplane in front of the gas pumps at 11:45 AM the heat was blistering. We could hardly wait to get refueled and into the air-conditioned office.

We contacted Jim Winterringer and shortly he and his wife and son arrived and drove us into town for lunch at a very nice family restaurant. They seemed very interested in the history of the Cub. He was not a pilot but his father had used the airplane to hunt coyotes and he recalled that he had not particularly enjoyed these excursions as the low flying had scared him.

After lunch we drove back to the airport and he had a good look at the Cub and photos were taken for the record.

It was getting near 2:30 PM and we planned our next leg. We decide on Pierre, South Dakota and then to Mobridge but on further consideration it seemed better to go to Huron and then to Mobridge, which would make two flights of approximately, equal duration rather than a long and then a short one. My map was getting a little cluttered with course lines but I thought I could keep them straight in my mind.

Climbing back into the aircraft the heat was overwhelming and one had to be very careful to avoid touching the metal parts that had been exposed to the sun. (Another advantage of a wooden airplane.)

As soon as the engine started there was some relief from the heat but this seemed to me to be the hottest spot on the trip so far. We got into the air at 2:35 PM. The heat must have addled my brain because the details of that takeoff seem to have disappeared from my mind entirely and I don't even recall the runway direction we used.

The country between Yankton and Huron contained nothing of note. It was flat, open country and the only town we passed was Mitchell to the west of us about 70 miles along the way. We landed at Huron a little after 4:00 PM and as I taxied up to the ramp I noticed two people come out of the office to service the Cub. One was obviously a young man but the other was very tall, slim with short dark hair and from where I was I couldn't tell if it was a man or woman. If it was a woman she must have been nearly six feet tall. As I shut down this person came over to me. At the first words I realized that it was a woman. She seemed quite amused by all the flying wires on the Fly Baby and looked at me as if I were Wilbur Wright.

It turned out that this was a family operation and I was dealing with the mother. After getting gas and oil we went into the relative coolness of the office. There I witnessed the final acts of the family's Beagle dog. It had just finished rolling over and playing dead and then the son told it to answer the phone whereupon it jumped up onto the chair, put its front feet on the desk and removed the receiver with its teeth and dropped it on the desk top. Glen and Kay informed me that it had quite a repertoire and it certainly seemed to be quite alert.

Our departure was somewhat delayed when my engine refused to start. I was reluctant to prime it as Continentals flood very easily when hot and then a long wait is in order. Our perseverance paid off but poor Glen had worked up quite a sweat by the time it decided to keep running and then he had to go and start the Cub. Fortunately it didn't give him the same problem and started quite readily. I suppose my rich carburetor setting and his lean setting along with the temperature were taking effect as we moved into higher country.

We were in the air by 5:35 PM and set course for Mobridge, South Dakota, 130 miles to the northwest on the Missouri River.

The course lay over mostly open country with relatively few landmarks in the way of towns and populated areas. The air was smooth and somewhat cooler as evening approached.

After about two hours in the air we saw Mobridge. It was on the inner curve of a bend in the Missouri, which was quite wide at this point. The setting sun added considerable beauty to the scene. We landed on the single strip and backtracked to the ramp and tied down for the night.

As it was after 7:00 PM there was no one on duty so refueling would have to wait until morning. We found a phone in the building to close our flight plan and a notice saying that after normal operations the procedure was to phone the local sheriff for transportation to town. This we did but he must have been busy stamping out crime in some other part of town as we got no response. We finally gave up on the sheriff and phoned a taxi which took us to a very nice motel with an indoor swimming pool.

After a long, hot day that pool had number one priority and in a matter of minutes we were enjoying a refreshing dip.

Having cleaned up and changed the next order of business was the evening meal. We were a little late for the motel dining room so we took a stroll down the main drag in the hopes of discovering a likely eating establishment.

We discovered what appeared to be a local nightclub with tables around a dance floor and a western band entertaining. They assured us that they could feed us so we sat down. I had the feeling that the food would be on the order of a fast food outlet. Not so. A very attractive salad bar was set out and excellent steaks followed. The entertainment was also enjoyable and we strolled back to the motel feeling satisfied and at peace with the world.

The next morning we had breakfast in the motel coffee shop which overlooked the large expanse of water that was the Missouri River. Pictures and brochures about the lobby of people holding large fish gave us the impression that Mobridge was quite a gathering spot for the fishing fraternity and indeed quite a few cars and trucks with boat trailers were in evidence.

We took a taxi to the airport and did our preflight inspections and fueling which had not been possible the night before due to our late arrival.

The FBO gave us quite a cordial welcome and insisted on taking pictures of us beside our aircraft. Apparently he photographed all visiting aircraft and kept them in an album. It occurred to me that either there were not too many visiting aircraft or it was a good way to track down delinquent accounts. Oddly enough, a fellow pilot later told me that he had seen my picture on a wall in the airport in Mobridge, South Dakota.

We watched a Piper Pawnee spray plane take off. He must have been fully loaded as he burned up the whole runway before staggering into the air. He made a shallow turn and came back along the east side of the field still not more than 100 feet above the ground. I thought it was because he couldn't climb but I guess those fellows never operate much above that altitude because of the nature of their work.

It was soon our turn. We didn't have to taxi too far as what little wind there was from the northwest and the taxiway joined the runway as its southeast end.

We did our runups and the Cub was off and climbing. I pulled into position and started my takeoff roll and soon we were airborne and heading out over the Missouri which was about a half mile wide at this point. Glen said later that he wondered if I would circle for altitude before attempting to cross the water but at that time the thought never entered my head. Perhaps its what I should have done but I was so taken with the beauty of the sunlight sparkling off the blue water that the engine did not go into "automatic rough". When you are flying over relatively flat land any break in the topography is refreshing, especially a river the size of the Missouri.

We flew parallel to the Missouri for about 40 miles with the river on our right and at Standing Rock, where we could see the airstrip on its west bank; it turned away gradually to the northeast.

After another 40 mile we could just see Bismarck on the horizon to the northeast and now we were over some desolate dry and rocky country.

It didn't occur to me at the time but later I realized we were probably flying over an area filled with missile silos and no doubt we were being tracked very carefully on somebody's radar screen.

Our course crossed the highway from Bismarck at New Salem and I noticed we had about 40 miles to go to our destination at Beulah, North Dakota. Half an hour later I started looking for Beulah and, according to the map, the strip ran northwest-southeast almost paralleling our course. We seemed to be bucking a headwind so we should be set up for a straight-in approach.

We continued on but saw no sight of an airship. A tall smokestack appeared on our left in the distance but still no airport. We were now flying into a shallow valley and I was in line astern of the Cub and about mile behind. The Cub was sinking lower so I followed hoping they had seen something I hadn't. Eventually I saw it. A paved strip right in the bottom of the valley with the town off to the right.

We not only landed into the wind but slightly uphill so the roll out was short. We backtracked to the taxiway, taxied up to the ramp and shut down. The time was 12:30, two and a half hours from Mobridge.

The main business at this airport was crop spraying and we carefully studied a helicopter set up for this purpose.

After refueling we turned our attention to getting some lunch. The FBO gave us the keys to a courtesy car that looked like it had been resurrected from the local auto wrecker.

I managed to get it started and we drove into have a look at "beautiful downtown Beulah, the Lignite capital of the world". We found a restaurant on the main drag and went in.

It was somewhat spartan and the luncheon special was some strange Ukrainian dish. We felt adventurous so we ordered it. I won't comment on it other than to say it was somewhat of a disappointment.

Back at the airport we prepared for our next leg of the journey to Estevan, Saskatchewan. As this involved border crossing we also had to make arrangements to clear customs.

It was now the hottest part of the day and we could hardly wait to get airborne. We fired up, taxied out and backtracked to the end of the runway and did our runups. This was going to be a little tricky. We were fully loaded with gas, the day was hot, the runway was uphill and we had to climb out of the high end of the valley.

The Cub started to roll and was airborne fairly soon but I knew my rate of clime wasn't going to be as good as theirs. The one thing in my favor was the field elevation which was only 1790 feet. I took a deep breath and opened the throttle and the Fly Baby rose to the occasion. She took about one half of the runway and then she was off. I leveled off to get full revs and then put her into the steepest climb that I dared. Fortunately it was more than sufficient and we were able to clear the high ground at 2276 feet by a safe margin.

About 20 miles out of Beulah to the northwest our track crossed Lake Sakakawea, which is formed by the dam on the Missouri at Garrison. This lake must extend over a mile upstream and was several miles wide at our point of crossing. The lake ran almost due east and west at this point and as we were angling across it to the northwest this made it even farther. Believe me, I made sure I had lots of altitude this time before I started across. Fortunately my headphones fitted fairly snugly so I was not aware of any "automatic rough" on the part of the engine.

The lake turned and ran north and south some ten miles west of us and we paralleled it for about 35 miles crossing the tips of two inlets. We then left the lake as it turned west again and flew over some very sparsely populated country. There were very few landmarks other than a few clusters of small lakes. As we approached these the Cub seemed to be drifting off to the east and I could see no obvious reason for this. I checked my map and the course line ran right across the center of two small lakes that I could identify straight ahead. I normally stayed to the right of the Cub and a little low in the 4 o'clock position but if I was to stay on course it meant moving to the left of the Cub.

I decided to stay on course because sooner or later they would have to come back on track and we would link up again or so I thought. The Cub kept widening the distance between us until soon it was just a dot in the sky. I was now in a dilemma as to what to do. There weren't many land-marks in this part of the country so it was important to stay on course. If I went chasing after the Cub I would use up precious fuel and there was always the chance that we would both get lost. I tried the radio without success and Glen was trying to reach Estevan to see if they had heard from me, again without success. I was up sun from him and now so far away that he had lost me but I could still just barely see him.

We were now about 40 miles out of Estevan and slowly but surly the gap between us began to close and I began to breathe a little easier. Soon I was back on station again and we began our descent into Estevan.

The familiar triangle with the World War II hangers appeared in the distance and we were cleared for a straight-in approach on runway 30. It was now 4:00 PM, the day was hot and the wind was gusty so the approach and landing was a little tricky. We taxied in to the ramp. The Cub pulled up to the pumps and I parked across the taxiway on the grass. We sat in the aircraft and waited for the Customs Officer. We didn't have to wait long as he appeared very shortly. While he was checking out Glen and Kay I watched grasshoppers by the hundreds jumping all over the aircraft. They made a constant drumming as they landed on the fabric of the wings.

The Customs Officer soon came over to me and said I could get out. I had been sitting for two and a half hours in that cramped cockpit and had a little difficulty accomplishing this as rigor mortis seemed to be setting in. He found this quit amusing which got us off to a good start. He was interested in the Fly Baby and didn't see where I could possibly have any room to smuggle anything so our business didn't take long. We went into the flight office and completed the necessary forms then he wished us good trip and drove off in his car.

We refueled and had a cup of coffee and walked around a bit to get the kinks out. I made sure the canopy on the Fly Baby was closed as I didn't fancy a swarm of grasshoppers for company on the next flight.

Our next stop was Regina and we dug out the WAC chart (World Aeronautical Chart) for Saskatchewan and Alberta and drew our course lines and marked off ten miles increments. It was 130 miles to Regina, which translated to about two and a half hours flying time taking the headwind into consideration.

As I taxied out to take off it occurred that the cement taxiway must have been the original wartime installation as my wheels practically fell down the gaps between them and the tumbleweeds growing out of them resembled small trees. Fortunately the runway had had more recent care and the takeoff was accomplished without incident.

Just after takeoff we crossed a small lake and a gravel pit complete with crusher. A power failure on takeoff here would be a complete disaster.

Our course paralleled both the highway and the railway on up to Weyburn where we could see the old air force base and the triangular patterns of runways. From Weyburn it was about an hour's flight to Regina with nothing of note on the ground except highway and railway. We were cleared for a straight-in approach on runway 30. This time we were able to find our way into the Regina Flying Club with no problem and parked and tied down for the night.

We were a little weary, as this has been our longest day having been in the air for nine and a half hours. As a result we were glad to see Ann Hamilton and once again enjoyed the hospitality of her home.

About this time Glen informed me that they had decided to stay in Regina an extra day to rest up and give Kay and Ann a chance to visit. We had worked as a team for so long that the realization that I was going to be on my own for the rest of the way came as a bit of a shock to me. It was a comfort to have that other aircraft in sight and even though they couldn't have done anything to prevent a forced landing they could at least marked the site and directed assistance if it were necessary.

That night there was a thunderstorm and heavy rain that woke me up once or twice but by the morning it seemed to have cleared up. I phoned for a weather check for the area between Regina and Swift Current and was told I could expect a headwind and the possibility of light, scattered showers.

We were at the airport by 9:00 AM and I untied the aircraft and did my preflight. After filling my flight plan I strapped in and Glen gave me a start. This was the last time I could except service. I called tower and got a taxi clearance to the end of runway 26 and from here on I was on my own. Everything checked out on the runup so I signified that I was ready for takeoff and got my clearance. I lined up and opened the throttle and soon I was airborne and climbing.

I headed down the highway for Moose Jaw which was only 40 miles away and as I was now on my own I could cruise about 10 miles an hour faster. I was there in a little over half an hour so I figured I was bucking a headwind as I had been told by the weather office. I passes well to the north of the town to stay out of the control zone of the CFB (Canadian Forces Base) to the south of Moose Jaw and then set course for Swift Current.

The highway curved to the north about this point so I decided to cut the corner and fly a straight line for two reasons. I had a headwind that I wanted to compensate for and the sky was looking a little dark to my right over the highway so there could possibly be some showers in the area. It was not a well-defined cloud and appeared to be thin enough to see though and the edge of it, which was even thinner, was in my path. No real problem here or so I thought. About 40 miles west of Moose Jaw I ran into light rain but visibility was still good so I held my course. The rain became heavier. I was flying with the canopy open and decided to test the old adage that you couldn't get wet in an open cockpit as the rain would pass over you with the airflow. I can definitely state that this is not true, at lease not at the speed I was traveling, as I was getting soaked. So I closed the canopy and watched the streaks of water slowly climb up the windscreen. It was now raining quite heavily which was surprising as the visibility was still quite good and the clouds seemed to be just a thin mist where I was.

The back of my propeller was painted a flat black to cut down on reflections and all of a sudden I saw a white arc on it which steadily grew wider. When it reached about twelve inches it stopped. I knew that this probably meant that the fiberglass had separated from the prop. I hoped that it had torn right off as I recalled the case of a Pietenpol with the same problem and the cloth had stayed on and reduced the prop efficiency to the point where the aircraft could not maintain altitude. I immediately started checking the terrain below me in the event that I had to make a forced landing. I wade over a dry alkali lake called Lake Chaplin on the map and although it looked level I was not sure whether the soil would be firm or soft. I decided if need be I would stay clear of the lakebed. There was not a sign of human habitation or civilization for miles in each direction so it would be a long walk for help if I went down.

I looked over at the highway about twenty miles to my right but the rain was much heavier in that direction so I thought I would be better to just hold my heading and stay where I was. I seemed to be maintaining altitude and the damage didn't seem to be getting any worse. I don't think I have ever felt so all alone. My radio would be of no help as I was out of range. I just had to trust to luck that nothing worse would happen until I got to Swift Current, which was still 50 miles away.

As the minutes passed and the situation did not get any worse and I began to think I might survive. The rain seemed to be getting lighter and soon it stopped altogether and the sky brightened somewhat. Slowly, agonizingly, the distance between Swift Current and me closed and fortunately the airport was ten miles this side of the town. Finally I could see it and dialed 122.3 on the radio and called in. Runway 30 was the choice which was almost a straight-in approach and I had only alter course slightly to the right to line up with the runway. It seemed to take forever to get there. I thought it was my state of mind and my hurry to get there but I soon realized that the wind was quite strong. As I got lower I ran into quite a bit of surface turbulence and a wing would drop quite suddenly and viciously. This was all I needed after what I had been through but I concentrated hard on this landing trying to be ready for the next gust. Now I was over the threshold and I kept a little more power on than usual to help maintain control. One or two minor buffeting gusts and then I felt the wheels make contact. Back with the throttle and ahead with the stick to pin her down and with that wind I was soon stopped. I pushed in the Carb heat, did a 180-degree turn and backtracked to the taxiway at the threshold.

Swift Current is not the most attractive airport in the world but it sure looked good to me as I taxied up to the pumps and shut the engine off.

My first action was to examine the prop. A strip about twelve inches wide on both the front and the back was gone on one blade and a similar one about eight inches wide was missing on the other. The wood on the leading edge had the appearance of having been sandblasted with fairly deep pits in it and the remaining fiberglass would soon suffer the same consequences with continued operation.

It was clear that I wouldn't be flying until some emergency repairs were done. As long as the strong, gusty wind kept up that would also ground me so I knew my project for the afternoon would be. I started to work on the prop but I could hardly stand up against the wind so I asked if I might be able to move the aircraft inside as I would probably be staying overnight. They were most cooperative and as there was lots of room I was soon in the hangar with the door closed although the wind kept banging it back and forth against the tracks.

I got out my tape and epoxy kit. Started at the trailing edge of the prop on the outboard side of the damaged area I ran a strip of masking tape around the leading edge and ended on the trailing edge on the other side. I then ran another strip over lapping the first and kept doing this until the damaged area was covered, working inward and creating a shingled effect, each layer holding the next down. I repeated the procedure on the other blade and when I had finished I mixed up the epoxy and smeared as smooth a layer as I could over the whole taped area.

I figured this would be hard by morning to keep the tape in place until I could get home. It may not have been an approved repair but I figured it would hold together for one more day and that's all I needed.

I now needed a ride to town as it was nearly ten miles and I was about to phone a cab when the flying instructor at the club said he would be going at five o'clock and would give me a ride. I took him up on his kind offer and settled down in the lounge to wait. This was the same room we had waited out the wind in on the way down so the surroundings were now becoming quite familiar.

About 4:30 PM he came in and said I could get a ride with two fellows who were going into town so I got my gear together and went out. They appeared to be a couple of older farmers who had just dropped in for a visit and were going back home so I climbed into their pickup and off we went.

They asked me where I wanted to go and I had been told to stay at the Best Western Motel as they supplied transportation and could probably get a ride to the airport in the morning. This proved to be difficult to find and they spent a long time searching for it. I was getting quite embarrassed by this time and said that any motel would do when suddenly we spotted it.

I thanked them for their kindness and went into the office to check in. I said I just wanted a unit for the night. Something small and not too fancy and that is what I got. I don't think I have ever been in a smaller motel room but it was entirely adequate and the price was right.

After I got cleaned up I phoned my wife to let he know that I was going to be delayed another day and that I was spending the night in "Beautiful Downtown Swift Current".

There was a small restaurant close to the motel where I had a pleasant meal and then I wandered over to a shopping center where I purchased some tape and epoxy just in case I had further problems.

I went back to the motel, had a shower, watched a program on TV and then sank into the arms of Morpheus.

The next morning I woke up greatly refreshed and looked out of the window. Blue sky as far as I could see. I looked for flags or smoke to check wind and there wasn't much sign of that.

I quickly shaved and packed and got breakfast at the local coffee shop and then went to check out and reap the benefits of the free limousine service to the airport.

The man behind the desk apologized but said that he was all alone that morning and couldn't leave the desk so I had to call a cab after all.

My first concern was that state of my repair job. I thought I had used a fast drying epoxy but it was still pretty tacky. It would have to do as I couldn't wait around forever. I could check it again at Medicine Hat and if necessary do whatever was required to patch it up.

I rolled the airplane out of the hanger and parked her in the grass at the edge of the concrete apron.

I then went over to the next hanger and checked in with flight services. The forecast looked good with only a moderate headwind so I filed a flight plan and left. I dug out one of my tie-downs, screwed it into the ground and tied the tailwheel firmly to it. I reached into the cockpit and turned the valve at the bottom of the tank to the 'on' position. Then I pulled out the primer handle and gave it a couple shots. Making sure the switches were off I went around and pulled the prop through a half dozen times. Then I went back, set the throttle and turned the switches on. I stood behind the prop on the right side and hung on to the flying wires with my left hand meanwhile placing my left foot in front of the right wheel to act as a chock. I snapped the blade down once she fired right off the bat. I hopped up on the wing walk and reduced the throttle to 800 rpm and checked the oil pressure gauge—35 pounds—OK. After throttling back I untied the tail, stowed the tie-down, climbed in and fastened my seat and shoulder harness.

The two areas of tape and epoxy on the prop flashed in the sunlight with a strobe effect. I taxied out to the end of runway 30 and turned into the wind for my runup. Everything OK I announced my intentions on the radio and took off at 9:00 AM for Medicine Hat 130 miles away. Once in the air everything felt good and it was obviously a nicer day weather wise. This time the highway veered to the south on my left towards Gull Lake while I cut the corner to the north. There were a few more lakes both wet and dry dotting the countryside, the sky was blue and everything was running smoothly.

About 75 miles en route I looked to the left to spot Maple Creek. Perhaps the light conditions were a little different but I was never so conscious of the increase in elevation to the south and west. The land rose quite markedly to Maple Creek and beyond it to Cyprus Hills and west towards Medicine Hat. I made a mental note to keep an eye on the altimeter.

I was flying open cockpit again and was quite conscious of the smell of exhaust fumes. As the stacks exit below the cowl there was obviously a leak in the system somewhere but with all that fresh air rushing by I wasn't too concerned.

I crossed Bitter Lake and then flew along the south shore of Many Island Lake. I was about 30 miles from Medicine Hat and things were going quite smoothly.

I got clearance for a straight-in approach to runway 27 and began my descent. It was now 10:30 AM and as I was approaching over the gravel pit I prepared for rough air from a combination of differential heating and surface turbulence. I was not disappointed and my landing consisted of one bounce before I got it under control. I taxied into the fuel pumps and shut down.

My first concern was the condition of the propeller. The epoxy, which had not quite hardened, had run in small rivulets towards the tip having been thrown outward by centrifugal force. However, it was not serious and there was no sign of the tape lifting or separating so it appeared that I would make it home without repairs.

I checked with flight services and the weather looked good for the final leg of the journey with only a slight headwind to contend with. I filed my flight plan and headed back to the aircraft.

I had to tie down again to start because very few ramp personal know how to hand prop nor are they willing to and I can't say that I blame them as it can be dangerous.

I taxied out to the end of runway 27, did my runup and after announcing my intentions on the radio on 122.2 I took off for the last hop.

Sunshine prevailed and I felt relaxed and was enjoying the flight. Suffield passed under my right wing and I could see Lake Newell coming up on the left. After passing to the north of Brooks and their airstrip I noticed the highway veered off to the west. I passed right over Rosemary and the next landmark should have been Deadhorse Lake at Hussar. I knew better than to look for a body of water but found Hussar with no trouble. I noted the compass heading as I was going to run out of landmarks pretty soon and just held the heading. I could see Standard off to the left and then I was over open country with no distinctive landmarks. Only forty miles to go now to Acme but although I searched the country beneath me I could see nothing that looked familiar. Eventually grain elevators dotted the horizon so I knew I should be approaching the railway coming out of Calgary through Irricana, Besecker and Acme. I held the compass heading and eventually right over the nose appeared the farm with its three runways.

I dropped lower and passed over the field noting the position of the windsock. Wind from the southeast. Runway 13. I was running a little over my ETA (Estimated time of arrival) so I was anxious to get down and close my flight plan. I very seldom had occasion to use 13 so I was not too familiar with its condition and the hump in the middle. Just as I touched down I hit the hump and found myself twenty feet in the air again. I suppose I should have gone around again but I was in such a hurry to get down I tried to ride it out. She hit very hard, bounced and then stayed down. I was disgusted with myself. The last landing and I blew it.

I taxied in to the hanger and shut down, removed my helmet and climbed out. I hurried over to the house to close my flight plan and found the door locked and no one around. In desperation I went back to the aircraft and tried to reach Calgary Tower on the radio but, of course, I was out of range. I then got into my truck and drove north to next farm. There were only two children at home and they had probably been told not to let strangers in the house. They finally, reluctantly, allowed me to use the phone so I was able to close my flight plan.

I drove back to the hanger and put the aircraft away. While I was tying it down I noticed the flying wires were slack so I stepped back to check the alignment. As the flying wires attach to the axle hub I suspected a bent axle from the hard landing and sure enough there was considerable misalignment. There was also a discoloration around the front of the cowling so I suspected a blown exhaust gasket.

The airplane as now due for its hundred hour inspection so I added these items to the list of things to be fixed.

As I drove home to Calgary I reflected on the details of trip and decided that it had been one of the highlights of my life. It certainly did wonders for my piloting, navigation and confidence in my ability to deal with unexpected situations and I met some wonderful people in the bargain.

▼

EXTRA FUEL

Not long ago, the most wondrous thing about the general aviation industry in the U.S. was that it wasn't dead yet. How quickly matters change! Now, 'gen av' is on the brink of a new and promising era. Despite the naysayers and prophets of doom who continue to predict its demise the light plane industry is emerging from the 'Dark Ages' of the 1980s and 1990s, heading into a 21st Century renaissance. And nowhere was that transition more than evident at the Experimental Aircraft Association's 45th annual Convention and Sport Aircraft Exhibition.
◆ **Aviation Week & Space Technology; Aug. 11, 1997** ◆

▼

Patty Wagstaff

Being a Performer

The first time I went to Oshkosh was 1984. Except for a couple of small airshows I'd flown in Alaska, it was the second airshow I had ever seen. It was also the year I flew my first contest at Fond du Lac, the following week. I had just discovered aerobatics the year before, and had joined the IAC, the EAA, and had watched my first airshow and was about to compete in my first contest.

Needless to say, I was in hog heaven. I went to the IAC booth and met Eric Meuller, the great Swiss aerobatics pilot who had just flown across the pond in his little single-engine Robin. I watched performers like Bob Lyjack, Earl and Paula Cherry, the French Connection and Bob & Pat Wagner. But, the neatest part of my first Oshkosh experience was when I was sitting at a picnic bench eating a sandwich and a group of airshow performers were sitting at a nearby table. I couldn't help but overhear their conversation, and of course, I leaned a little closer just so I could. I don't remember anything particular they were saying, but it was just really exciting to hear these people talk about the airshow and their lives. From the first airshow I saw, I knew I was on the wrong side of the fence, and that I would be an airshow performer one day.

The first time I flew Oshkosh was in 1987. Duane Cole gave me a good reference and helped get me in. I was flying my all time favorite airplane at the time, a white with red and blue starburst stock 260 hp Pitts S-2S. That was the year that I met Curtis Pitts.

For a performer, flying Oshkosh is very special and unique. At most airshows we figure about 20% of the population are pilots. At Oshkosh, it's like 100% of the people are pilots or at least enthusiasts. You are really flying in front of your peers. I am always a little nervous my first flight at Oshkosh, and I'm rarely nervous flying an airshow.

They used to have a rule that no matter what your "Low Altitude Waiver" was, the first time you flew Oshkosh it had to be at 500' AGL. I liked that rule and wish it still stood. I had a 0 altitude waiver at the time, and was proficient enough to fly lower, but I stayed at 500' and hoped they would like my flying enough to invite me back the next day, when I could fly my usual lower show. Of course, something had to happen and my smoke system stopped working. I was very upset, thinking I'd made a big fool of myself. Now I know better. People really didn't even notice.

I haven't had any hair-raising experiences at Oshkosh. If I make a mistake, I don't want it to be in front of 800,000 of my peers. I'm very cautious to try to make a good impression!

I've met so many memorable people at Oshkosh, and people that I see there year after year...Aviation people like Curtis Pitts, Chuck Yeager, Burt and Dick Rutan, Richard Bach, and others with an interest in aviation like Michael Dorn, the actor, who flies his own jet. He held a pole for me one year. I always ask the VIP's to hold a pole for me. One of the top dogs from the NTSB owes me a hand, as do a couple of FAA guys. I want to get them out there on the runway while I can legally give them a low-level buzz job!

Oshkosh is rather overwhelming for me now. There are a lot of demands of the performers and they seem to increase every year. Not that we mind, but it takes a lot of logistics to make it all work—the briefings, flying the airshow, forums, talks, and raffles, book signings, autograph sessions and interviews. I sometimes feel like a zombie at the end of the day. I'm sure everyone thinks the performers are out there closing the bars every night, and there are days you do, but some nights I find myself searching for peace and quiet at 9 PM. Boring, and don't tell anyone about that, okay? It might ruin my image.

The most wonderful things happen at Oshkosh. People who were kids ten years ago come up to me and tell me that I encouraged them to pursue their dream to fly and now they are in the Air Force or pursuing a career as an airline pilot. These kids are adults, so it makes me feel old, but really good too! Another great thing that happens is all the fathers that bring their daughters over to meet me. They are encouraging them to pursue their dreams and not settle for anything less. I'm proud to be seen as a role model for the kids and that is one of the best things that Oshkosh has given me personally.

EAA treats the performers well. We know we'll have a decent hotel room or two, a nice rental car, a laid-back performers party and overall good treatment. It's great to see the same group of volunteers year after year. It's like coming home for Thanksgiving and seeing your long lost family. You can't say that for all airshows. Oshkosh is a hard show to get into and the performer that gets to fly Oshkosh feels they "made it" and joined an elite club. Only the best need apply.

There's a spirit to Oshkosh that is hard to define. It is uplifting. It encompasses a lot of things—family, kind-heartedness, sharing and encouragement. I wish everyone could feel the spirit of volunteerism that's evident at the Convention. I wish we could export it. If we could we'd have world peace!

▼

Mike McKeig

Oshkosh or Bust

I've never been to Oshkosh. It seems I've always had too much to do in my life and didn't have time. Career, family, money—all seemed like perfectly legit reasons for not going. Yet, I really expected to have been there by now. After all, airplanes and flying are in my blood. They have been as far back as I can remember. Some of my very earliest memories are of flying with my grandfather. I had a logbook before I could ride a bike. My uncle was an Air Force pilot and a real inspiration to a little boy that loved flying machines. My dad even flew until a bad experience with a Piper Cub put an end to his flying days. I've always devoured anything related to flying.

You probably know someone like me. Maybe you even see it in yourself. We're easy to pick out in a crowd. Someone will mention anything remotely related to flying and off we go. Our spouses will just roll their eyes, knowing they've lost us. Next thing you know, we're hand-flying our way into oblivion. People like us should really get a regular dose of Oshkosh or seek professional help.

What's so special about Oshkosh anyway? For one thing, isn't "Oshkosh" code for the event of the year? When you mention Oshkosh, if the other person doesn't say "Where?" or "What do jeans have to do with it?", you're talking to an aviation fan. You don't have to explain you are referring to the Experimental Aviation Association's annual fly-in event. You just know.

From what I've read, watched on TV and gleaned from friends who've been to Oshkosh, it's special. Sure, we've all heard it described as the world's busiest airport with airplanes of every shape, color and size, but it is more than that. At Oshkosh, you get to see some of the rarest sights around. There are the only remaining examples of their type, fleets of warbirds, awesome military craft and some of the finest looking "regular" airplanes in the world. There is room for every type of airplane imaginable. If it can fly, someone will be interested.

Being EAA's home, Oshkosh is where the spirit of innovation in aircraft design lives. It is the place where you bring out your best stuff to show the world. Okay, so maybe we don't need another crackpot trying to sell the world a "flying car", but it is also where you see the work of true everyday geniuses. Who knows which of them will be the next Wright, Northrop, Johnson or Rutan?

The performances at Oshkosh have more of a spark to them. Perhaps it is because the pilots all know they are performing for the greatest number of knowledgeable people who will ever see them at one time. Of course, they all know it is okay if everything isn't perfect. Their friends would never give them a hard time about one tiny mistake, would they?

Oshkosh offers new ideas, tons of cool airplanes and great performances. What else could there be? For me, perhaps the greatest attraction is the people who attend. Some of the best times of my life have involved flying and being around other airplane people. Oshkosh seems like a kind of family reunion. The people who go to Oshkosh have a common love of aviation. What better group of people could there be for an airplane nut to hang out with and discuss the day's events? I imagine my biggest problem would be finding time to sleep.

My hat is off to all of you who make the time to go to Oshkosh, especially the regulars. Upon reflection, I have no excuse and will be joining you shortly. If you've ever had the urge to go to Oshkosh, why not give it a shot?

It is a holiday for the soul.
◆ **Russian aviation official visiting** ◆

▼

Harold Bickford

A Builder of Model Aircraft

Another facet of what EAA can mean to people

As a builder of model aircraft, for me Oshkosh becomes an incredible display of types both well known and obscure. In terms of obscure aircraft, two designs that were long sought favorites have been at Oshkosh; the Bugatti 100 which of course hangs in the museum and the Stinson A tri-motor which was there in '98.

I had wanted to find a Stinson A since I was a kid in the 50s and had built a model of one. The Bugatti search came about from an article in Air Progress in 1973 which was subsequently lost. Both searches culminated at Oshkosh because EAA people desire to preserve and perpetuate aviation. Modelers such as myself benefit from this just as do those who are working on or flying the full-scale versions. Being able to sit on the doorstep of history in this way is an experience that people should not forego.

The Fly-In has become sport aviation's mecca, where pilots can also attend workshops on amateur plane construction. Homebuilders around the world dream of flying their planes to Oshkosh.
◆ **Malcolm McConnell, Reader's Digest, August 1998** ◆

▼

Mark Welter

Spousal Warning!

If your spouse is an airplane nut and you didn't go to Oshkosh with him/her, I have bad news for you! Letting an aviation nut alone at Oshkosh is somewhat akin to letting a frat house have an unsupervised party in a beer brewery.

If your spouse returned home dragging a U-Haul trailer behind his car and is acting evasive about its contents, you need to do some investigating. To the untrained eye, an unassembled kit airplane is a hard thing to identify. He/She may tell you that it is just some old scrap metal and stuff. There are a couple of good ways to tell if it is an airplane. Look first for three tires, one of which is smaller than the other two. Next, look for some little black gizmos that may have things like "ALTITUDE", "AIRSPEED", or "HOBBS" printed on them. These are all evidence of an airplane kit. If you should find a little black gizmo with "MACH" or "LBS/THRUST" written on it, you really have big time troubles. Immediately go to the phone, call your insurance agent and take out a multi-million dollar life insurance policy on their life. And don't ever look in the garage again!

I checked through a book on kit planes and found that the prices range from $2500 to $406,000. The one for $406,000 did include the motor.

I managed to get several parts of my kit into the trunk of my Thunderbird. My wife thinks the planes I got are for a little pedal powered airplane for the grand kiddies. Boy, will she be surprised when she sees them taxiing down the sidewalk!

ABOUT THE AUTHOR

Jill is the daughter of world famous aviator Dick Rutan who, along with Jeana Yeager, piloted the Voyager experimental aircraft on its non-stop, unrefueled, around-the-world flight in 1986 establishing several Absolute Aviation Records.

Along with her obligations as a full time wife and mother of two beautiful daughters, Jill lives her own dreams as an aviation writer and private pilot and actively supports her husband's exciting career as a test pilot in the United States Air Force.

Jill can be reached at her web site

www.lookingskyward.com